OECD *Economic Surveys*
Electronic Books

The OECD, recognising the strategic role of electronic publishing, will be issuing the OECD **Economic Surveys**, both for the Member countries and for countries of Central and Eastern Europe covered by the Organisation's Centre for Co-operation with Economies in Transition, as electronic books with effect from the 1994/1995 series -- incorporating the text, tables and figures of the printed version. The information will appear on screen in an identical format, including the use of colour in graphs.

The electronic book, which retains the quality and readability of the printed version throughout, will enable readers to take advantage of the new tools that the ACROBAT software (included on the diskette) provides by offering the following benefits:

❑   User-friendly and intuitive interface
❑   Comprehensive index for rapid text retrieval, including a table of contents, as well as a list of numbered tables and figures
❑   Rapid browse and search facilities
❑   Zoom facility for magnifying graphics or for increasing page size for easy readability
❑   Cut and paste capabilities
❑   Printing facility
❑   Reduced volume for easy filing/portability

Working environment: DOS, Windows or Macintosh.

Subscription:	FF 1 800	US$317	£200	DM 545
Single issue:	FF 130	US$24	£14	DM 40

Complete 1994/1995 series on CD-ROM:

	FF 2 000	US$365	£220	DM 600

Please send your order to OECD Electronic Editions or, preferably, to the Centre or bookshop with whom you placed your initial order for this Economic Survey.

OECD
ECONOMIC
SURVEYS

1994-1995

MEXICO

ORGANISATION FOR ECONOMIC CO-OPERATION AND DEVELOPMENT

ORGANISATION FOR ECONOMIC CO-OPERATION AND DEVELOPMENT

Pursuant to Article 1 of the Convention signed in Paris on 14th December 1960, and which came into force on 30th September 1961, the Organisation for Economic Co-operation and Development (OECD) shall promote policies designed:

- to achieve the highest sustainable economic growth and employment and a rising standard of living in Member countries, while maintaining financial stability, and thus to contribute to the development of the world economy;
- to contribute to sound economic expansion in Member as well as non-member countries in the process of economic development; and
- to contribute to the expansion of world trade on a multilateral, non-discriminatory basis in accordance with international obligations.

The original Member countries of the OECD are Austria, Belgium, Canada, Denmark, France, Germany, Greece, Iceland, Ireland, Italy, Luxembourg, the Netherlands, Norway, Portugal, Spain, Sweden, Switzerland, Turkey, the United Kingdom and the United States. The following countries became Members subsequently through accession at the dates indicated hereafter: Japan (28th April 1964), Finland (28th January 1969), Australia (7th June 1971), New Zealand (29th May 1973) and Mexico (18th May 1994). The Commission of the European Communities takes part in the work of the OECD (Article 13 of the OECD Convention).

Publié également en français.

Table of contents

Box

Tables

Annexes

Statistical annex and structural indicators

Figures

BASIC STATISTICS OF MEXICO

THE LAND

Area (sq. km)	1 967 183	Inhabitants in major cities	
Agricultural area (sq. km) (1990)	394 600	(thousands) (1990)	
		Mexico city	15 048
		Quadalajara	3 044
		Monterrey	2 651

THE PEOPLE

Population (thousands) (1992)	85 628	Employment (thousands) (1993)	23 251
Inhabitants per sq. km (1992)	43.5		
Annual population growth (1980-1992)	2.2		

PRODUCTION

Structure of production		GDP (in US$ billion (1993)	361.9
(per cent of total) (1994)		GDP per capita (in US$)	3 967.9
Agriculture	6.9	Gross capital formation	
Industry	30.2	(per cent of GNP) (1993)	22.6
of which: manufacturing	21.2		
Services	62.9		

THE GOVERNMENT

			Chamber
General government consumption		Composition	
(per cent of GDP) (1994)	11.8	of Parliament (1995)	Senate	of Deputies
Federal Government capital expenditure		PRI	95	300
(per cent of GDP) (1994)	2.4	PAN	25	119
Federal government revenue		PRD	8	71
(per cent of GDP) (1994)	17.1	Other	0	10
Government debt (1994)			
(per cent of GDP)	24.9		

FOREIGN TRADE

Exports of goods and services		Imports of goods and services	
(per cent of GDP) (1994)	13.1	(per cent of GDP) (1994)	18.3
Main exports (per cent of total) (1994)		Main imports (per cent of total) (1994)	
Manufactures	69.8	Intermediate goods	61.2
Petroleum products	21.4	Capital goods	22.6
Agriculture	7.7	Consumer goods	16.2

THE CURRENCY

Monetary unit: New Peso.	Currency units per US$, average of daily	
	figures:	
	Year 1994	3.418
	July 1995	6.111

Note: An international comparison of certain basic statistics is given in an annex table.

This Survey is based on the Secretariat's study prepared for the annual review of Mexico by the Economic and Development Review Committee on 10 July 1995.

•

After revisions in the light of discussions during the review, final approval of the Survey for publication was given by the Committee on 27 July 1995.

•

The previous Survey of Mexico (as a non-member country) was issued in September 1992.

Introduction

When the Committee reviewed Mexico for the first time in July 1992 (as a non-Member country at that time), the economy was in its fourth year of expansion, and the rate of inflation – though still high relative to that of its main trading partners – was steadily falling. Public finances were under control. A consensus-based incomes policy was in place. And the government was well engaged in a process of structural reforms aimed at strengthening private initiative and creating an open competitive economy. Despite notable successes that had been recorded, the risk of excessive real exchange rate appreciation was stressed in the 1992 *Economic Survey* and attention was drawn to the worrying resurgence of a large current account deficit. The trend decline in domestic saving – notwithstanding the large increase in public saving – was seen as a cause for concern in the face of the investment boom, which was welcome inasmuch as it supported the much-needed modernisation of the economy.

1993 saw a pause in the widening of the current account deficit, as uncertainties about the ratification of the North American Free Trade Agreement (NAFTA) depressed economic activity. But in 1994, an election year, the economy started growing again, and the current account deficit rose sharply, while the Chiapas uprising and a series of political shocks undermined investors' confidence. By December, when the new government took office, the margin of manœuvre for policy makers had become very narrow. A new wave of capital outflows precipitated a currency crisis, which was then followed by several months of turbulence in foreign exchange and financial markets.

Part I of this Survey reviews economic developments and the forces which led to the December crisis, and assesses the role of economic policies. The magnitude of the financial crisis that developed in the wake of the peso devaluation has called for rigorous corrective actions. The authorities adopted a series of stabilisation measures, and international financial support has been arranged to help Mexico meet its foreign obligations. The various steps taken to stabilise the economy and reduce financial market volatility are discussed in Part II, which also sketches out the short-term outlook. Part III of the Survey examines macro-economic policy requirements facing the authorities in the years ahead, once the immediate objectives of stabilisation are attained.

Boosting sustainable growth over the medium term will require that structural reform continues in a number of key areas, notably privatisation, competition policy, prudential supervision, the agricultural sector and the labour market. Part IV presents an overview of the progress made in these areas and attempts to evaluate the need for further reforms. One of the major problems that the government has been tackling energetically – but which is likely to be exacerbated by the large adjustment cost of the stabilisation measures and the fiscal tightness that is required – is poverty: precarious living conditions for large segments of the population, linked with skewed distribution of income and uneven access to basic social services. These issues and policies pursued in these areas are discussed in Part V. Finally, the main findings of the Survey are summarised and policy conclusions are drawn in Part VI.

I. Origins and evolution of the current crisis

Overview

For several years after 1988, the Mexican authorities pursued a prudent macroeconomic policy combining strict control of public finances and monetary policy which was aimed at achieving convergence to inflation rates of its main trading partners, mainly the United States. Macroeconomic policies were implemented within the context of a publicised effort of social concertation (the Pacto) which included a flexible incomes policy. Wide-ranging structural reforms were undertaken, most notably privatisation, deregulation, and the outward reorientation of the economy, illustrated most recently by the signing of NAFTA. The stance of macroeconomic policy in 1993 and 1994 marked a change from the previous period. Economic activity in 1993 was subdued, partly as a result of uncertainties about NAFTA ratification which held up decisions to invest, and the Mexican authorities moved to a more expansionary policy stance. The gradual run-down of the budget surplus and a considerable expansion of loans by state-owned development banks provided a stimulus to economic activity. Despite high real interest rates, commercial bank credit to the private sector also grew rapidly and this helped domestic demand and imports to recover in 1994. The use of a firm exchange rate commitment to anchor monetary policy in the pursuit of disinflation succeeded in keeping inflation on a downward course. Consumer price inflation fell from three-digit levels in 1988 to some 7 per cent in 1994. Disinflation was accompanied by large capital inflows from 1990 to February 1994, and by a significant appreciation of the real exchange rate.

Despite notable achievements in reducing inflation and making the economy more flexible, Mexico's economic performance over the last few years was less than satisfactory in several respects. Real GDP growth at close to 3 per cent in 1988-94 was insufficient either to recoup losses in per capita GDP suffered

3

during the stabilisation period that followed the debt crisis of 1982 or to reduce the underutilisation of the rapidly growing labour force (Figure 1). To some extent the slow growth may have been inevitable as the economy adjusted to the deep structural reforms undertaken and was subjected to real exchange rate appreciation. Despite modest growth, however, the current account deficit widened persistently, to almost 8 per cent of GDP in 1994, reflecting insufficient domestic saving relative to the investment efforts of Mexican firms seeking to meet increased competition. While helping to deepen financial markets, financial deregulation contributed to the decline in the ratio of private saving to GDP until 1993, as banks competed to gain market shares, often extending consumer credit and housing loans without adequate risk assessment. This led to a deterioration of private-sector balance sheets and poor quality of banks' loan portfolios. In 1993 and 1994, public saving decreased and, although private saving recovered somewhat, it was insufficient to finance investment, so that the current account deficit continued to widen. The current account deficits were financed predominantly by large inflows of foreign capital, portfolio investment being the largest component, while the flow of foreign direct investment was increasing steadily. The large size of short-term inflows created a situation of vulnerability to changes in financial market perceptions.

Interest rates abroad rose in 1994, particularly in the United States, and the attractiveness of investments in emerging markets diminished generally. In Mexico, in addition, political shocks starting in January 1994 with the Chiapas uprising and continuing throughout the year undermined investors' confidence. When the peso came under attack in March, following the assassination of the leading candidate for the Presidential elections, Luis Donaldo Colosio, heavy intervention to support the currency induced considerable losses in official foreign reserves. Money-market interest rates were raised but did not reach a sufficient level to prevent a shift out of pesos as the already significant problems in the banking sector limited the margin of action of the central bank. Thereafter, central bank reserves remained broadly unchanged, the shock waves being largely accommodated through increased issues of dollar-indexed securities (Tesobonos). In December, investors' worries about political instability and economic prospects in Mexico intensified, triggering a new wave of capital outflows. On 20 December, with the level of reserves unsustainably low, the government widened the exchange-rate band, allowing the peso to devalue by

Figure 1. **KEY ASPECTS OF ECONOMIC ACTIVITY**[1]

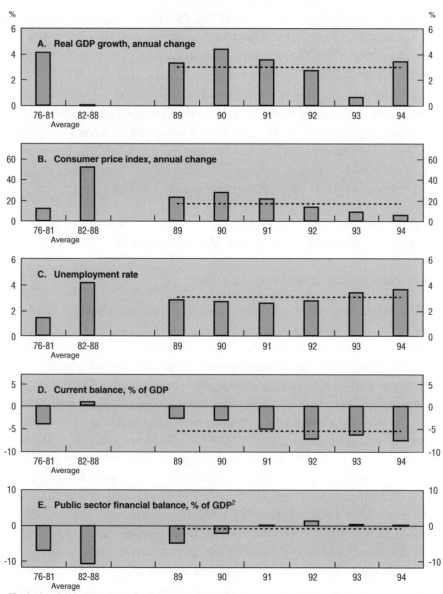

1. The broken line is the average for 1989-94; average annual changes are calculated from 1975 to 1981, 1981 to 1988 and 1988 to 1994 respectively.
2. Public sector financial balance excludes receipts from privatisations and financial intermediation of the development banks.
Source: OECD, INEGI and Ministry of Finance.

15 per cent. Two days later, under unabating pressure against the peso, the exchange rate was allowed to float freely. By the end of December, the peso had fallen by around 30 per cent from end-November; and the downward move continued in early 1995.[1] At the same time, interest rates increased sharply, and the stock market crashed.

In the following, economic developments up to the December crisis are first reviewed. The authorities' macroeconomic policies are then discussed with a view to assessing their role in the episode. A final section describes the unfolding of the crisis until March 1995, when the announcement of a large package of international liquidity support and a reinforcement of the government's stabilisation programme began to rebuild financial market confidence.

Economic developments up to the December crisis

Slow growth despite a recovery in 1994

Real output growth, which was close to zero in the second half of 1993, rebounded in 1994 peaking at rates over 4½ per cent in the second and third quarter from a year earlier. Real GDP expanded by 3½ per cent in 1994 as a whole, with particularly rapid output growth in the non-tradeable sectors – construction, electricity, transport and financial services (Table 1). The economic recovery in 1994 may be viewed as the resumption of growth trends which had been under way for a number of years and were interrupted in 1993 because of uncertainties about the ratification of NAFTA. Consumer spending and business investment, which had been held up until after the entry into force of NAFTA, picked up at the start of the year. Nevertheless, at 2.1 per cent per year on average, the expansion of real GDP in 1993-94 was well below the average annual growth rate recorded over the 1988-92 expansion period, and this was despite stimulative macroeconomic policies. In 1994, fiscal policy was eased and the impulse to activity was reinforced by buoyant credit from publicly-owned development banks which was already rising at high rates in 1993.

Households' consumption had stagnated in 1993, while private saving rose somewhat in relation to GDP. In 1994, the lowering of import tariffs after NAFTA and relatively low import prices due to the real appreciation of the peso stimulated spending on consumer durables, cars in particular. Employment gains

Table 1. **Demand and output**

Percentage changes, 1980 prices

	1991 Current prices[1]	1988-91[2]	1992	1993	1994
Demand					
Private consumption	621.2	5.9	3.9	0.2	3.7
Government consumption	78.0	2.0	2.3	2.0	2.5
Gross fixed capital formation	168.5	9.2	10.8	−1.2	8.1
Public	39.4	3.7	−5.0	−3.8	8.9
Private construction	51.3	4.8	14.0	6.5	5.3
Other private	77.7	15.1	149.0	−0.4	10.2
Final domestic demand	867.7	6.1	5.1	0.1	4.5
Change in stockbuilding[3]	25.3	1.1	0.7	−0.3	0.0
Total domestic demand	893.0	5.4	5.1	−0.3	4.5
Exports of goods and services	119.5	3.5	1.7	3.7	7.3
Imports of goods and services	147.4	19.2	20.9	−1.3	12.9
Change in foreign balance[3]	−27.8	−1.6	−2.8	0.9	−0.9
GDP at market prices	865.2	3.8	2.8	0.7	3.5
Output					
Agriculture, forestry, fishing	78.5	1.6	−1.4	2.6	2.0
Mining (including petroleum)	18.1	1.0	1.8	0.9	1.6
Manufacturing	192.5	5.7	2.3	−0.8	3.6
Construction	36.2	3.8	7.8	2.8	6.4
Electricity	13.1	4.4	3.0	4.2	7.7
Commerce	214.2	4.1	3.6	−1.3	2.8
Transport and communication	76.5	5.5	7.6	3.3	7.8
Financial services	108.4	3.5	3.7	4.7	5.2
Community services	150.5	2.3	0.6	1.2	1.9

1. Billion new pesos.
2. Annual growth rate.
3. As a percentage of GDP in the previous period.
Source: INEGI.

and real wage increases together boosted household incomes sufficiently to allow the recovery in consumption, as well as a further rise in the private saving rate.[2] Over the period 1993-94, real consumption growth, at an average rate under 2 per cent, was well below the rate recorded over the previous five years, and insufficient to allow an increase in per capita consumption overall.

The small rise in the ratio of private saving to GDP in 1993 marked a break in the steady decline of the previous years. From 1988 to 1992, private saving had fallen cumulatively by 9 percentage points of GDP, while public-sector saving became significantly larger over the period (Table 2). According to a recent study[3] the fall in private saving recorded between 1989 and 1992 can be ascribed to two main factors: *i)* the increase in the value of financial assets (used as a proxy of wealth); *ii)* the consolidation of public finances. The increase in the value of financial assets may have reflected improved expectations of future incomes which, along with the increased ease in obtaining credit following financial market liberalisation, stimulated spending by both households and enterprises. Fiscal consolidation can affect private saving in several ways. First, increased taxes lower disposable income of the private sector. Second, higher public saving can reduce private saving by reducing the current income level through the multiplier effect. Third, reduced public-sector borrowing increases the funds available to the private sector, thereby stimulating its spending. Finally, increased government saving may reduce private agents' incentives to save by feeding expectations of lower taxes in the future. Econometric results suggest that about half of the rise in government saving is offset by a fall in private saving (*i.e.* if public saving rises by 100 pesos, private saving falls by 50). Thus, over the long run the net impact of fiscal consolidation on domestic saving is positive.

In 1993 and 1994, public-sector saving fell significantly, while the ratio of private saving to GDP rose in 1993, remaining unchanged in 1994. Total national saving, which increased slightly in 1993 as a percentage of GDP, fell back in 1994; but the aggregate investment/GDP ratio rose, owing to the pickup in both public and private sectors.

Table 2. **Savings and investment**

Percentage of GDP

	1988	1989	1990	1991	1992	1993	1994
Gross capital formation	20.4	21.4	21.9	22.4	23.3	23.2	23.5
National saving	19.3	18.8	19.2	17.8	16.1	16.7	15.8
Private[1]	17.5	14.8	11.7	9.7	8.4	10.7	10.7
Public[2]	1.8	4.0	7.5	8.1	7.7	6.0	5.1
Foreign saving	1.1	2.6	2.7	4.6	7.2	6.5	7.7

1. The figure is obtained by subtracting public savings from national savings.
2. The public sector comprises federal government and enterprises under budgetary control. The estimate is adjusted by the inflationary component of interest payments of the public debt.
Source: OECD, INEGI and Ministry of Finance.

Improved business expectations after NAFTA and strong export results led to a recovery of private investment in 1994, after a standstill in 1993.[4] However, the positive impact of these factors was probably dampened by higher real interest rates after March 1994 and repeated political shocks. The growth of investment was helped by the expansion of foreign direct investment – largely related to NAFTA – which amounted to more than US$8 billion in 1994, compared with 4.4 billion the previous year. Public investment which had fallen over the previous three years – partly the result of the privatisation of public enterprises – expanded by almost 9 per cent. Total investment growth – by 4 per cent per year on average – seems modest, compared with the annual average growth rate during 1988-92.[5] Capital goods imports surged in 1994, after a significant decline in 1993, while domestic production of machinery and equipment nearly stagnated (Table 3).

Owing mainly to a rise in Mexico's export market growth in 1994, which essentially reflected stronger growth in the United States, Mexico's export volumes increased by over 7 per cent, a significantly faster pace than the average in the previous ten years.[6] However, the pick-up in activity and lower customs tariffs brought about a surge in the volume of imports, and the real foreign balance was a net drag on GDP growth, as has been the case every year since 1988, except during the 1993 downturn (Figure 2).

It is not unusual for an economy undergoing deep and broadly-based restructuring, as is the case with Mexico, to experience a relatively long period of slow growth while adjusting to these changes. This has been illustrated by several

Table 3. **Indicators of investment activity**

Volumes, percentage changes from same period of previous year

	1993	1994	1993				1994				1995
	Average	Average	Q1	Q2	Q3	Q4	Q1	Q2	Q3	Q4	Q1
Gross fixed investment	−1.2	8.1	4.9	−1.8	−5.3	−2.4	3.0	7.9	11.7	9.9	−18.4
Construction added value	3.2	6.4	7.7	2.2	−1.1	4.0	3.6	8.0	11.1	3.5	−7.3
Domestic production of machinery and equipment	−5.5	0.5	2.2	−10.7	−8.2	−4.2	−7.4	0.5	4.0	5.3	−41.2
Imports of capital goods	−6.4	20.6	1.3	0.5	−11.4	−14.0	13.7	16.0	21.6	31.0	−23.0

Source: INEGI.

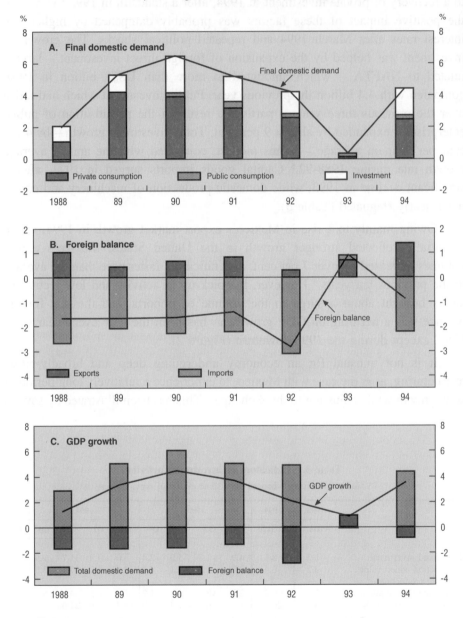

Figure 2. **CONTRIBUTIONS TO REAL GDP GROWTH**

As a percentage of real GDP in the previous year

A. Final domestic demand

Final domestic demand

Private consumption   Public consumption   Investment

B. Foreign balance

Exports   Imports

Foreign balance

C. GDP growth

GDP growth

Total domestic demand   Foreign balance

Source: OECD.

years of poor growth record in New Zealand after wide-ranging structural reforms were carried out.[7] Increased exposure to international competition and liberalised financial markets tend to be associated with increased import penetration and a widening of the current account deficit. In Mexico, this has been reflected in the continued negative contribution of the real foreign balance since the economy started to grow in 1988. More exports are likely to be generated in the future by the rapid growth of investment over the late 1980s and early 1990s and import substitution may be progressively enhanced, but significant lags are involved before the new production capacity comes on stream. Meanwhile, imports of investment goods have been boosted. At the same time, as has been the experience in many low-income countries, a wider range of consumer durables has become available through the lowering of import barriers, causing a surge in imports. These effects have been compounded by the real appreciation of the currency over several years (see section below).

Persistent labour market slack

Modest economic growth has meant that the pace of job creation has been too slow to absorb a rapidly rising workforce. Although there is a lack of comprehensive statistics, data on insured employees – the best available indicator for the formal sector – suggest that in 1994 the net creation of jobs was slightly positive, as the number of insured workers picked up in the second half of the year (Table 4). Net job creation was concentrated in the service sector while the manufacturing sector again recorded significant job losses as a result of industrial restructuring.[8] By contrast, employment in in-bond industries (''maquiladoras'') grew by about 10 per cent in 1994, in parallel to an increase in both the number of plants and the sector's real value added. After expanding vigorously for several years, the sector now employs some 600 000 workers, 7 per cent of the total number of insured workers.

The small expansion of employment in 1994 should be viewed against contrasting trends of slowing population growth (below 2 per cent per year since the start of the decade), but still rapid expansion of the labour force (3.5 per cent per year), due to the age structure of the population and rising female participation rates. Thus, every year more than one million new entrants need to be absorbed in the labour market. When growth and job creation in the formal sector of the economy prove insufficient, excess labour finds employment in the infor-

11

Table 4. **Labour market indicators**

	1991	1992	1993	1994	May 1995[1]
	Thousands	Annual percentage changes			
Labour force[2]	31 229	3.8	3.8	–	–
Men	21 630	3.7	3.7	–	–
Women	9 599	4.1	4.1	–	–
Total insured employment[3]	11 016	2.5	0.2	1.1	–1.6
of which:					
IMSS, permanent	9 773	2.3	0.4	1.4	0.0
Manufacturing	3 080	–0.5	–3.2	–0.8	–0.5
Construction	241	10.1	6.2	2.9	–10.0
Traded services	1 634	3.2	1.1	1.4	–0.4
Personal services	1 589	2.8	2.4	1.9	0.5
Other	1 240	5.0	4.5	4.7	2.9
Employment in manufacturing[4]	–	–3.8	–7.3	–4.8	–5.6
	Percentages				
Urban areas[5]					
Participation rate[6]	53.3	53.8	55.2	54.6	54.3
Men	73.9	73.9	74.9	74.5	73.6
Women	34.5	35.6	37.1	36.5	36.8
Open unemployment rate	2.6	2.8	3.4	3.7	5.5
Men	2.5	2.7	3.2	3.6	5.3
Women	2.9	3.2	3.9	3.9	5.7
Unemployment rate (wider definition)[7]	4.2	4.8	5.5	6.1	8.1

1. January-May 1995, compared with January-May 1994; the data for manufacturing employment refer to January-April.
2. INEGI, *National Survey of Employment*, 1991 and 1993.
3. Based on registers of social security institutes.
4. INEGI, *Monthly Survey of Industry*.
5. The National Survey of Urban Employment only covers a limited number of areas (initially 16, raised to 32 since 1992 and 39 since 1994).
6. "Economically active" population as a percentage of population 12 years and over.
7. Open unemployment plus people who gave up seeking employment, are no longer included in the labour force, but are available for work.
Source: INEGI, IMSS.

mal sector. While this phenomenon has been particularly conspicuous in recession years, the growth of the informal sector is not exclusively counter-cyclical. The sector includes a network of micro-enterprises of between 1 and 5 employees which has been expanding over the years.[9] In 1994, the recovery in economic activity, in manufacturing in particular, was too fragile – and perhaps too short – to allow enough jobs in the formal economy to be created, and the number of

Figure 3. **OPEN UNEMPLOYMENT RATE AND OTHER LABOUR MARKET INDICATORS**

As a percentage of labour force 12 years and over

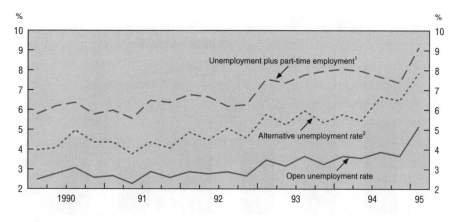

1. Part-time refers to employees working less than 15 hours a week.
2. Includes those who stopped searching for a job but are still available for work.
Source: INEGI.

people engaged in informal activities did not decrease. The open unemployment rate in urban areas – a poor indicator of available capacity on the labour market in a country with a dual labour market and no unemployment insurance – continued to rise in 1994. The number of people engaged in part-time work, a component of unemployment in a wider sense, declined towards the end of the year (Figure 3).

Inflation and competitiveness

Under generally tight monetary policy based on exchange-rate commitment, inflation, as measured by the consumer price index, declined from over 100 per cent in 1988 to 10 per cent in 1993. It continued to slow in 1994 to 7 per cent (both in average and end-of-year terms) – 3 points below the 1993 average. Service prices, which largely reflect wage cost developments, increased by 7½ per cent over the twelve months to December, only slightly above average inflation and a significant reduction from a year earlier (Figure 4). The deceleration was parallel to that of labour costs, suggesting that the margin of unused capacity on the labour market continued to have moderating impact on wages

13

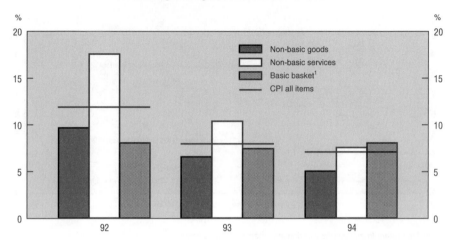

Figure 4. **CONSUMER PRICES**

Percentage changes, December to December

- Non-basic goods
- Non-basic services
- Basic basket[1]
- CPI all items

1. Basic goods and services, of which some supplied by the public sector (gasoline, electricity).
Source: Banco de México.

(Figure 5, Panel A). In the manufacturing sector, unit labour costs (defined as nominal labour costs per unit of output) were roughly stable on average in 1994 because of large productivity gains.[10] A continued deceleration in prices of goods exposed to international competition (whose weight in the CPI is about one-third) reflected not only these favourable labour cost trends but also two specific factors: first, lower import tariffs following the entry into force of NAFTA (the mechanical effect is estimated by Mexican authorities at 0.6 percentage points for 1994); second, increased competition both from abroad, putting pressure on Mexican producers, and from inside, as the rising market share of supermarkets put pressure on margins of more traditional retail outlets.

The further narrowing of inflation differentials with Mexico's main trading partners during 1994 and the 10 per cent fall of the peso in March 1994 (within the fluctuation band) meant that the international price competitiveness of Mexican manufactured products, which had been slowly deteriorating since the mid-1980s, remained unchanged from 1993 (Figure 6). During 1994, competitiveness improved, because of the peso depreciation within its band. The accumulated loss of competitiveness associated with the real appreciation of the peso

Figure 5. **REAL WAGES, LABOUR PRODUCTIVITY AND PRICE TRENDS**

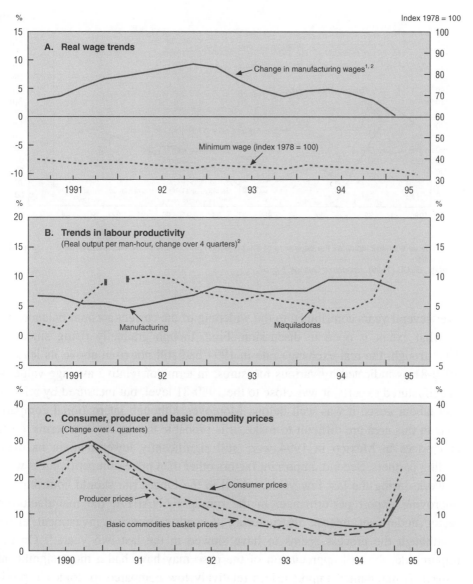

%   Index 1978 = 100

A. Real wage trends

Change in manufacturing wages[1,2]

Minimum wage (index 1978 = 100)

B. Trends in labour productivity
(Real output per man-hour, change over 4 quarters)[2]

Manufacturing

Maquiladoras

C. Consumer, producer and basic commodity prices
(Change over 4 quarters)

Consumer prices

Producer prices

Basic commodities basket prices

1. Wages, salaries and social benefits, based on INEGI monthly industrial survey. Year on year percentage change.
2. Moving average over 3 quarters.
Source: INEGI and Banco de México.

15

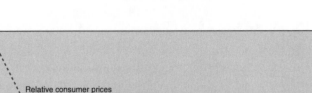

Figure 6. **MEXICO'S RELATIVE COMPETITIVE POSITION**

Indices in US$ terms

Note: The vertical line indicates the beginning of the projection period; a fall indicates improvement in competitive position.

Source: OECD (1995), *Economic Outlook,* No. 57.

over several years contributed to the widening of the current account balance, but to what extent is open to discussion. First, though gradually rising since the 1987 trough, the real exchange rate in 1994 had still not risen above its level in 1980-81 as indicated by various measures: in terms of relative average value of manufactured exports, it was close to the 1980-81 level, but measured by relative unit labour costs, it was well below. Moreover, although international comparisons in this area are difficult to make, it is probable that in absolute terms, costs and prices in Mexico in 1994 were still significantly lower than in its main trading partners. Second, important factors other than price-competitiveness were at work during the last few years, which in the longer run should contribute to improving export performance: in the run-up to NAFTA, the manufacturing sector underwent intense restructuring through a massive investment effort – although the process seems to have slowed in the last two years.[11] On the import side, the real appreciation of the peso may have had a more significant impact. It maintained import prices relatively low compared to domestic products, thus reinforcing the effect of structural changes (*e.g.* reduction of import tariffs and wider availability of new products for consumption), and facilitating import penetration.

16

A widening current account deficit

With the recovery in activity and still stronger ties with the world economy, Mexico's current account deficit widened to US$28.8 billion in 1994; in relation to GDP, this was slightly higher than in both 1992 and 1993. The steady increase of current account deficit in relation to GDP – it rose by 2 percentage points in 1991 and in 1992 – had come to a halt in 1993 because of the slowdown in aggregate demand. The widening of the current account deficit reflects a sharp rise in the trade deficit, which reached a record US$24 billion in 1994, 6.6 per cent of GDP (excluding the in-bond sector or maquiladoras).[12] The maquiladoras surplus, which had steadily increased over the years, amounted to US$5.8 billion in 1994. Net oil exports, at US$7.4 billion, were unchanged from 1993. Merchandise trade flows accelerated with the entry into force of NAFTA: while exports (in dollar terms) grew by 15.3 per cent, imports rose by more than 20 per cent.

The rise in the trade deficit in 1994 essentially reflected changes in volumes, as terms of trade remained virtually stable.[13] Imports continued to rise in relation to aggregate demand (including exports), as a result of both structural and cyclical factors, reaching 16 per cent compared with 10 per cent in 1989, the first year of the upswing. The forces at work in the early years of the recovery were strengthened by the favourable climate created by NAFTA. Imports of consumer durables recorded hefty growth rates, the stabilisation period of the 1980s having left a considerable backlog of pent-up demand; but imports of investment goods and intermediate products were also booming, driven by the export-led recovery.[14] In addition, import demand is likely to have been stimulated by relatively low prices, which reflected the strength of the Mexican peso in real effective terms until April, as well as cuts in customs tariffs.

Growth of merchandise export volumes appears to have accelerated from some 9 per cent in 1993 to over 12 per cent in 1994. However, this expansion occurred in the context of even stronger growth of Mexico's export markets (Figure 7).[15] The losses in price competitiveness accumulated in the previous years seem to have hindered Mexico's export performance; but the effect was attenuated by the structural changes that have improved Mexico's exporting capacity.

Despite the increase in maquiladoras' net exports, the balance of non-factor services remained roughly unchanged in 1994, largely as a result of the rise in freight and insurance payments. The positive balance in tourism widened as both

17

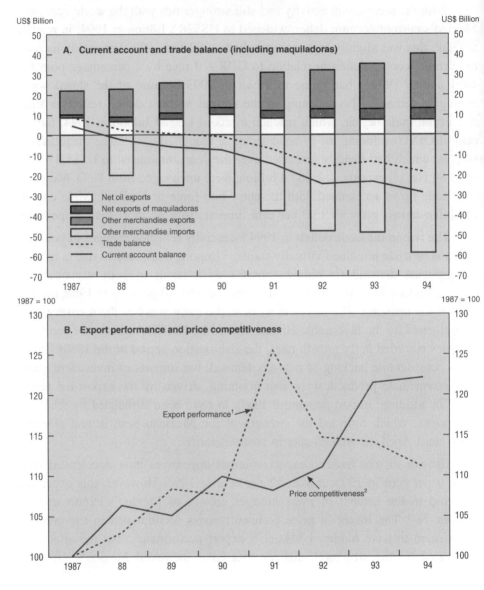

Figure 7. **FOREIGN TRADE, CURRENT ACCOUNT AND EXPORT PERFORMANCE**

A. Current account and trade balance (including maquiladoras)

US$ Billion

- Net oil exports
- Net exports of maquiladoras
- Other merchandise exports
- Other merchandise imports
- - - - Trade balance
- —— Current account balance

B. Export performance and price competitiveness

1987 = 100

Export performance[1]

Price competitiveness[2]

1. Ratio of Mexico's exports of manufactures to its main partners imports of manufactures in volume terms.
2. Relative export unit value of manufactured goods. A rise indicates a deterioration.
Source: OECD and Banco de México.

the deficit in border tourism narrowed and the surplus in non-border travel widened – a consequence of the expansion in the United States. The deficit in factor incomes increased, due to the rise in interest rates abroad and profit repatriation by foreign investors.

An increasing vulnerability

Until 1994, Mexico had no difficulty in financing its current account deficit. Net capital inflows, which had doubled to US$11 billion between 1989 and 1990, reached nearly US$30 billion in 1993. Foreign direct investment kept rising, though at a modest rate in 1992-93, as the breakthrough expected to result from NAFTA was yet to come (Table 5). On the other hand, foreign portfolio investment rose considerably, to US$17 billion in 1993, more than three times as much as foreign direct investment. Increased confidence in Mexican firms' growth

Table 5. **Balance of payments**

US$ billion

	1991	1992	1993	1994
Exports (fob)[1]	26.9	27.5	30.0	34.6
Imports (fob)[1]	38.2	48.2	48.9	58.9
Trade balance[1]	–11.3	–20.7	–18.9	–24.3
(as per cent of GDP)	(–3.9)	(–6.3)	(–5.1)	(–6.4)
Non-factor services, net	2.3	2.4	3.3	3.6
of which:				
Tourism	0.1	0.0	0.6	1.0
In-bond industries	4.1	4.7	5.4	5.8
Investment income, net	–8.6	–9.6	–11.4	–12.2
Transfers, net	3.0	3.4	3.6	4.0
Current account balance	–14.6	–24.4	–23.4	–28.8
(as per cent of GDP)	–5.1	–7.4	–6.4	–7.7
Capital account	22.8	25.6	29.5	9.9
Official capital	4.3	6.8	7.5	–0.2
of which: Official borrowing	–0.1	–4.0	–3.4	–1.6
Private capital	18.5	18.8	21.7	10.1
of which:				
Direct investment	4.8	4.4	4.9	8.0
Net external credit	8.6	2.5	6.2	2.4
Portfolio investment	7.7	8.3	17.0	6.1
Other (including errors and omissions)	–2.6	3.3	–5.9	–6.4
Change in reserves (increase = –)	–7.8	–1.2	–6.1	18.9

1. Excluding trade by in-bond industries.
Source: Submissions by national authorities.

19

potential, high nominal domestic interest rates and a predetermined exchange rate, were all factors behind the rise. Foreign borrowing essentially resulted from private-sector operations and, in particular, the placing of long-term bonds by the non-bank sector. Among public sector entities, development banks were major users of external funds in 1993, to finance priority sectors predominantly through commercial banks, which assumed the risk of each project (see below). In contrast the Federal government and other public sector entities, such as PEMEX, made net amortisations. Combining the public and private sector, net external debt fell steadily as a percentage of GDP, to 36 per cent in 1993, with the share of the non-bank private sector in the total narrowing significantly (Table 6).[16] In fact, total capital inflows were high enough in 1993 to push up foreign exchange reserves by US$6 billion – in December that year they amounted to over US$24 billion.

Table 6. **External debt indicators**

At end of period, US$ billion[1]

		1993	November 1994[2]	December 1994[3]	March 1995[4]
A.	**Total gross external debt**	127.6	137.0	136.5	145.4
		(35.1)	(38.0)	(58.1)	(61.7)
	Public sector[5]	78.7	85.8	85.4	87.5
	Commercial banks	23.0	24.1[6]	25.1	22.0
	Private non-bank sector	20.3	27.1[6]	22.1	20.5
	Banco de México	4.8	–	3.9	14.7
B.	**Public sector external debt**[5]				
	Gross	78.7	85.8	85.4	87.5
		(21.8)	(23.4)	(36.4)	(37.1)
	Currency composition				
	US dollars[7]	61.7	62.0	62.2	61.0
	Basket of currencies (IADB and IBRD loans)	30.2	28.8	28.2	20.5
	Japanese Yen	8.4	8.5	8.4	9.0
	Deutsche Mark	3.1	3.2	3.2	3.5
	French Franc	3.0	3.0	2.9	3.2
	Net	69.4	77.5	76.9	78.9
		(19.2)	(21.2)	(32.8)	(33.6)

1. Figures in brackets are expressed as percentage of GDP.
2. End-November figure, unless otherwise specified. Ratios calculated at current exchange rate (3.44NP/$).
3. Debt/GDP ratios calculated on the basis of end-December exchange rate (5.33NP/$).
4. Preliminary figures.
5. Public external debt does not include government securities issued on the domestic market, which are held by non-residents (shown separately in Table 9).
6. End-September.
7. Of which about US$32 billion correspond to restructured debt ("Brady bonds").
Source: Ministry of Finance.

With private capital inflows exceeding the current account deficit up until the first quarter of 1994, the situation was not seen as a cause for concern. In some ways, it could be interpreted as a healthy sign for the economy: the modernisation of the productive structure in the longer run would lead to an increased supply of both exportable and import-competing goods, thus allowing for a reduction of the deficit in the future. As the public sector was in surplus – albeit decreasing – the current account deficit reflected essentially private agents' decisions to save and invest. While national saving was falling as a share of GDP, the investment/GDP ratio increased by 3 percentage points of GDP over the 1988-92 period, mostly accounted for by private investment. But the size of the current account deficit and the predominance of short-term capital in total capital inflows to finance the deficit made Mexican policies vulnerable to changes in investor sentiment.

As before, a steady – and substantial – inflow of foreign capital was needed to finance the current account deficit in 1994. But net inflows fell abruptly after the Colosio assassination. Foreign investors, increasingly worried about economic prospects and political instability in the country, reduced the share of Mexican securities in their portfolios. Investment in equities and in government paper fell by US$6 billion between January and November 1994 from a year earlier. Other outflows, including unrecorded transactions, already substantial in 1993, doubled to US$10 billion in 1994, suggesting a wave of capital flight. On the other hand, foreign direct investment inflows surged, reaching a record US$8 billion over the same period – a very positive development in the eyes of the Mexican authorities, since foreign direct investment is not subject to sudden shifts in investor sentiment, hence is not volatile.[17] Nevertheless the size of portfolio investments over the past years created a situation of vulnerability to changes in financial markets' perceptions. As the year developed, waves of capital outflows occurred and, overall, the surplus on the capital account was cut to US$10 billion. The stock of net international reserves was drawn down in steps, by a cumulated US$12 billion from end-1993 to the start of December 1994, when the new president took office (see Figure 13 below).

Policies up to the December crisis

Fiscal policy

Mexican authorities made impressive progress in fiscal consolidation during the 1980s and early 1990s, meeting their targets of bringing the public deficit under control and reducing outstanding debt. By 1992, fiscal balance was achieved and total public debt (domestic and external) had fallen to 27 per cent of GDP, from 51 per cent in 1982.[18] The brunt of the fiscal effort, as reflected in the improved primary balance, was achieved in the late 1980s.[19] After 1990, public finances continued to improve, largely as a result of the fall in interest payments obtained from debt redemption using privatisation proceeds. An overall surplus of 1.6 per cent of GDP was posted for 1992.[20] As part of the government's strategy from the start of the 1990s, some of the savings on interest payments were redeployed towards spending on social development. As a consequence, the primary surplus was reduced, falling to 5.8 per cent in 1992 (about 2.3 percentage points below its 1989 peak) (Figure 8).

Developments in 1993 and 1994 marked a change from previous years. The public sector financial surplus was cut by half to 0.7 per cent of GDP in 1993, moving to a small deficit in 1994 – a cumulative run-down of almost 2 percentage points of GDP over 2 years. As interest payments fell again over the period, the cumulative reduction in the primary surplus was more substantial (at 3.2 percentage points of GDP). In 1993, non-interest expenditure, which was projected to rise only marginally, increased by 1.6 percentage points of GDP from the previous year.

The budget for 1994, approved at the end of 1993, aimed at supporting a recovery in real GDP growth to 3 per cent, through tax concessions equivalent to $1/2$ percentage point of GDP. According to budget projections, the fiscal position was to move to near balance, the primary surplus decreasing to 2.6 per cent of GDP, from 3.8 per cent in 1993 (Table 7). Given that the economy was going through a severe slowdown at the time the budget was prepared, capital spending was frontloaded. GDP growth in 1994 turned out to be slightly stronger than expected; nevertheless, the public sector financial balance moved into a small deficit (0.3 per cent of GDP), suggesting that there was some slippage in the implementation of fiscal policy. Although there are no estimates available of cyclically-adjusted budget balances, it seems likely that in 1994, had there been no discretionary action on the part of the government, the budgetary position of the public sector would have improved thanks to the rebound in economic activity. Thus, fiscal easing on a "structural" basis would have been larger in 1994 than the deterioration in the actual budgetary position suggests.[21]

Public sector revenues remained roughly unchanged in 1994 (just above 25 per cent of GDP). Although tax concessions together with cuts in several

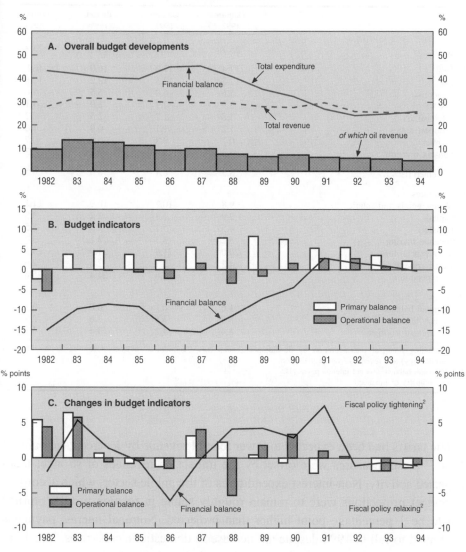

Figure 8. **BUDGET INDICATORS**[1]

Per cent of GDP

A. Overall budget developments

Total expenditure

Financial balance

Total revenue

of which oil revenue

B. Budget indicators

Financial balance

Primary balance

Operational balance

C. Changes in budget indicators

Fiscal policy tightening[2]

Primary balance

Operational balance

Financial balance

Fiscal policy relaxing[2]

1. Excluding privatisation receipts and financial intermediation by development banks; the financial balance is the "economic" balance according to the Mexican terminology; the primary balance is the financial balance less net interest payments while the operational balance is adjusted for inflation.
2. Tightening is measured as a rising surplus or narrowing deficit while relaxing is a falling surplus or widening deficit.
Source: Ministry of Finance, Banco de México.

Table 7. **Public sector accounts: budget and outturn**

Percentage of GDP

	Outturn 1992	Outturn 1993	Budget 1994	Outturn 1994
Revenue	25.7	25.4	24.4	25.2
Federal	17.4	17.0	16.0	16.8
Tax	12.3	12.5	12.2	12.6
Income	5.6	6.0	5.5	5.6
VAT	2.9	2.9	2.9	3.1
Excise tax	1.8	1.7	2.3	2.2
Import duties	1.2	1.1	0.9	1.0
Other	0.7	0.8	0.6	0.7
Non-tax revenue	5.2	4.5	3.8	4.2
Public enterprises	8.3	8.4	8.3	8.5
Expenditures				
Wages, goods and salaries	9.8	10.7	10.9	11.1
Capital	2.9	2.8	3.2	3.3
Transfers	4.5	5.1	5.5	5.5
Revenue sharing	3.2	3.3	3.1	3.3
Primary expenditure	20.0	21.6	21.9	23.0
Interest payments	4.2	3.1	2.6	2.6
Total expenditure	24.2	24.6	24.4	25.6
Balances				
Financial balance [1]	1.6	0.7	0.0	−0.3
Primary balance [2]	5.8	3.8	2.6	2.3
Government savings	4.4	4.2	3.4	3.8

1. Excluding financial intermediation by development banks (*i.e.* "economic" balance according to the Mexican terminology) and revenues from privatisation.
2. Financial balance *less* net interest payments.
Source: Ministry of Finance.

public tariffs had been expected to lower federal revenue by 1 percentage point of GDP,[22] these measures were offset by the impact on revenues of stronger-than-expected activity. Non-interest expenditures of the public sector, which according to budget projections were to remain roughly stable in relation to GDP, turned out to be 1 percentage point higher than projected. Nominal interest payments continued to fall in 1994 despite an increase in domestic interest rates, largely as a result of the switch from Cetes to dollar-indexed Tesobonos, on which the interest rate was considerably lower. As in the previous years, spending on social development rose significantly in real terms in 1994. Areas recording particularly high real growth were education, health and labour, Solidarity programmes[23] and rural development, especially direct support to rural workers (Table 8).

Table 8. **Public programmable expenditures by sector, 1994**

	Expenditure NP billion	Per cent of total	Real growth
Total	240.1	100.0	10.1
Social development	126.2	52.6	9.9
Education	54.3	22.6	10.1[1]
Health and labour	52.5	21.9	5.2[2]
Solidaridad	9.3	3.9	18.4
Urban development, drinking water and environment	7.1	3.0	35.7
Social provisioning programme	2.9	1.2	19.0
Rural development	15.7	6.6	41.5[3]
Communications and transport	15.6	6.5	21.7[4]
Energy	48.1	20.0	−1.8
Industry, commerce, fishing and tourism	10.6	4.4	−19.3
Justice and security	11.2	4.7	5.8[5]
Administration	12.7	5.3	89.4

1. The cumulative real increase from 1992 is 28 per cent, reflecting increases in both teachers' salaries and the number of teaching posts, productivity bonuses and higher spending on teacher training.
2. The cumulative real increase from 1992 is 15 per cent, reflecting wage increases of government health service employees, higher spending by the parastatal agencies on pensions, medication, medical supplies and child vaccination programmes, increased hospital infrastructure and creation of posts in new medical schools.
3. Reflects increased direct support to agricultural workers, irrigation works and loans and guarantees for agriculture.
4. Reflects road network development and maintenance.
5. The cumulative real increase from 1992 is 20 per cent, reflecting the creation of new posts in justice and national security administration and the fight against drug trafficking.
Source: Ministry of Finance.

Despite the gradual run-down of the primary surplus during the early 1990s, Mexico's fiscal position in 1994, in terms of both the primary surplus and overall financial balance, was one of the most favourable among OECD countries, while its public-sector debt was among the lowest. But the fiscal easing that took place in 1993 and 1994 gave a boost to economic activity at a time when the current account deficit was already reaching high levels. While this move worked counter-cyclically in 1993, it turned out to be pro-cyclical in 1994, and contributed to the deterioration in the current account. As the private saving/GDP ratio did not increase in 1994, the reduction in government savings widened the gap between domestic savings and investment that had to be financed externally.

Debt management

In line with previous years, government debt management in 1994 reflected two considerations: to lower the level of the debt, and to modify the structure of the debt in order to reduce service cost (Table 9). Over the past few years, as inflation and interest rates came down, the government retired longer-term bonds, mostly using Treasury bills of maturity of less than one year (such as Cetes) to finance its needs (Figure 9). In 1994, when it became difficult to place Cetes on the market, the authorities decided to switch to short-term dollar-indexed Tesobonos, on which the interest rate was considerably lower, the gap representing the market perceptions of currency or depreciation risk.[24] As a result of the shift, interest payments in 1994 fell again a little in relation to GDP, as projected in the budget despite the increase in Cetes rates after March. However, the switch also significantly increased the exposure of the government's fiscal position to exchange rate risk. The change also had implications for monetary policy, as it allowed domestic interest rates to remain lower than if the government had been financing most of its needs through non-indexed instruments. The Tesobonos issued were all short-term instruments (a year or less), which meant that in 1995 there would be significant amounts due to be rolled over. The rationale behind this choice, presumably, was that risk perceptions were expected to improve after the presidential elections in August, so that conditions would be favourable for roll-over or even a shift back to Cetes. By issuing dollar-indexed securities – and thus raising the stakes of a devaluation – the authorities were also signalling their commitment to maintaining the exchange rate stable.

Table 9. **Structure of government securities held by the public**[1]

End-December, US$ billion

	1993		1994	
	Total held by public	*of which:* by non-residents	Total held by public	*of which:* by non-residents
Total	38.7	21.9	29.6	19.6
Cetes	24.3	15.4	4.2	2.5
Bondes	4.5	0.8	0.6	0.0
Ajustabonos	8.2	4.4	2.8	0.5
Tesobonos	1.6	1.3	22.0	16.5

1. Excludes repurchase agreements. Cetes are Treasury bills with maturity of 1 month to 1 year (2-year Cetes have been issued since the end of 1993). Bondes are 1, 2, 10 year bonds. Ajustabonos are indexed to the CPI (3-5 year maturity). Tesobonos are dollar-linked securities payable in pesos (3, 6 month, 1 year maturity), not issued since February 1995.
Source: Ministry of Finance.

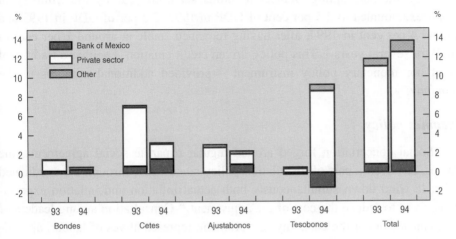

Figure 9. **COMPOSITION AND HOLDINGS OF GROSS PUBLIC DEBT**
As a percentage of GDP

Note: For description of various types of securities, see Table 9.
Source: Banco de México.

The role of development banks

The role of development banks compounded the public-sector financial situation and the markets' assessment of fiscal policy. These banks are government-owned financial institutions that provide financing to priority sectors, such as the export sector, local government infrastructure projects, small- and medium-size enterprises.[25] Two major changes in the way these banks operate were put in place in the early 1990s. First, the three larger ones became second-tier institutions, supplying funds to commercial banks and credit unions rather than dealing directly with retail customers; the others continue to deal directly with specific priority sectors. Second, in order to improve capitalisation, a system of portfolio rating was introduced that requires these institutions to hold reserves linked to credit risk. The accounting treatment of development banks was also modified. As of 1993, their financial operations were separated from the rest of the public sector accounts, a change that brings public accounting in Mexico more in line with international practice.[26] The move, however, may have been wrongly interpreted by financial markets as an attempt by the government to shift some activities "off-budget", despite the quarterly publication of relevant information by the National Banking Commission. The increase in development banks' credit outstanding, subject to limits set each year by the Ministry of Finance, amounted to 2.5 per cent of GDP in 1992, 3.2 per of GDP in 1993 and around 4 per cent in 1994, after having remained stable at around 1 per cent of GDP for several years.[27] This policy-driven credit creation – neither a traditional fiscal nor monetary policy instrument – provided additional stimulus to the economy.

Incomes policy

Social concertation forged around regular tripartite social agreements, the Pactos, has been a part of disinflation policy since 1987, through a co-ordinated effort to wind down simultaneously both actual inflation and inflation expectations, so as to reduce the cost of the adjustment.[28] Consultation among leaders of the main sectors of the economy (government, representatives of labour, agriculture and business) concerned the following main elements: the definition of the exchange rate regime, the setting of an inflation target, adjustments to public prices and tariffs, minimum wage increases and guidelines for private sector pay rises (Table 10). Over the years, public sector prices were maintained broadly

Table 10. **Pacto provisions from 1993 to 1995**

Signature Period covered	October 1993 1994	September 1994 1995 (initial)	January 1995 1995 (revised)
Exchange-rate band	Floor depreciated 0.004 peso a day	Floor depreciated 0.004 peso a day	Floating exchange rate
GDP growth (projection)	3 per cent	4 per cent	1.5 per cent
Inflation (Dec.-Dec.)	5 per cent	4 per cent	19 per cent
Minimum wage	Targeted inflation plus 2 per cent productivity gain	Targeted inflation plus 2 per cent productivity gain	7 per cent
Private wage settlements	To reflect targeted inflation and gains in productivity	To reflect targeted inflation and gains in productivity	To reflect targeted inflation and gains in productivity
Tax system	Cut in the top corporate income rate	Negative income tax on wages (up to 2 minimum wages). Tax incentives for corporate investment	Negative income tax on wages (up to 2 minimum wages).

Source: OECD, on information submitted by national authorities.

constant in real terms. The minimum wage, which was linked to target inflation, declined in real terms as inflation repeatedly overshot the targets. Contractual wages, which were determined more flexibly by settlements in the private sector, fared better.

In line with previous such agreements, the Pacto for 1994 (signed in October 1993) included a negotiated target for inflation (5 per cent), adjustments of public-sector prices and a 7 per cent increase of the minimum wage (of which 2 per cent on account of the projected increase in labour productivity for the economy as a whole). The Ninth Social Pact for Well-being, Stability and Growth, signed in September 1994 with the participation of the newly-independent Bank of Mexico as a fourth party, aimed at 4 per cent inflation and 4 per cent real GDP growth rate for 1995. Its goals became clearly unattainable in the wake of the December currency crisis.

Monetary policy

The orientation of monetary policy

Until the December 1994 crisis, monetary policy had for some years been oriented to maintaining some form of commitment with respect to the peso-dollar exchange rate. The most recent arrangement, established in November 1991, involved a system of fluctuation bands, the lower limit of which was depreciated at a pre-announced daily rate, with the upper limit held constant. This implied a gradual widening of the fluctuation band from an initial width of 1.1 per cent to around 15 per cent by late 1994. From early 1993, this system was supplemented by the daily announcement to the market of a narrower intervention band, aimed at establishing a trading range for that day, and supported by domestic market operations aimed at keeping monetary conditions consistent with the desired exchange-rate range. The system thus allowed somewhat more operational flexibility to the central bank than would have been the case with a formally fixed exchange rate, and increasingly so as the band was widened daily.

Notwithstanding this operational flexibility, the exchange-rate commitment implied a tight constraint on monetary policy over time. The permitted rate of depreciation of the band (initially 0.0002 pesos per day, or around 2 per cent annually, and revised to 0.0004 pesos per day in October 1992) only partially accommodated the inflation differential between Mexico and the United States until the end of 1993, and thus ensured that monetary policy was generally consistent with continued downward pressure on inflation. Real interest rates generally remained significantly positive from 1989 onwards and growth rates of the monetary and credit aggregates were substantially reduced over much of this period. However, these financial aggregates did not slow by as much as inflation itself and, in some cases, began to accelerate again in more recent years (see below for detailed discussion). The overall monetary policy strategy met with considerable success in reducing inflation to single figures by 1993. Market confidence in the exchange rate commitment increased, allowing interest differentials *vis-à-vis* the United States to narrow considerably, particularly in the period up to mid-1992 (Figure 10).

A general problem with using an exchange-rate commitment as a medium-term strategy for reducing inflation is that this will imply a rising real exchange rate during the time it takes for inflation to converge to international levels. As discussed earlier, Mexico's real exchange rate appreciated strongly during the disinflation period and, on some measures, approximately doubled between 1987 and 1994. Coming from a historically low base, some upward movement in the real exchange rate was clearly appropriate. Nonetheless, the trend real appreciation inevitably raised the issue (often referred to as the ''re-entry problem'') of how to deal with any over-valuation that might have accumulated by the time inflation convergence had been achieved. By 1994 a number of observers had identified this as a problem that needed to be addressed, although clearly the measurement of any real exchange-rate misalignment is subject to major uncertainties.[29]

For much of the early 1990s the upward trend in the real exchange rate reflected strong capital inflows, the counterpart to the high level of current account deficits. However, as discussed earlier, short-term portfolio investment formed an important part of the total inflows, and this meant that the exchange rate was highly vulnerable to a change in investor sentiment. Following a period of particularly strong capital inflows in late 1993 and early 1994, market confidence was shaken by a series of political shocks, including most importantly the assassination of presidential candidate Colosio in mid-March. These events brought about a re-evaluation by investors of the sustainability of the exchange rate under prevailing policies, and triggered massive capital outflows. Markets began to focus increasingly on the widening current account deficit and there were growing expectations that there would have to be either a realignment or a

Figure 10. **EXCHANGE RATE AND SHORT-TERM INTEREST RATES**

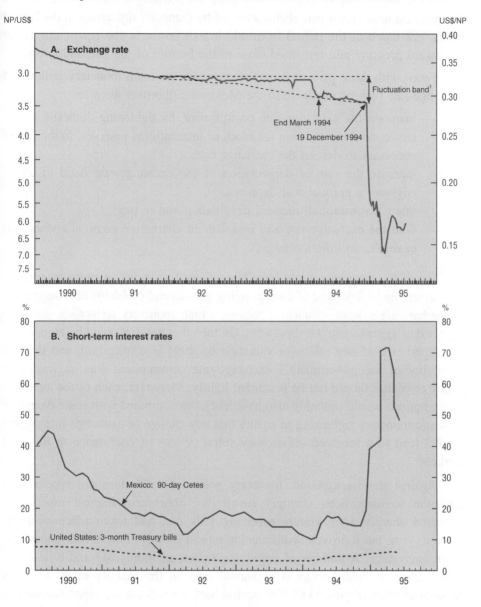

1. The upper limit of the fluctuation band was fixed at 3.05 NP/$; its lower limit was depreciated by 0.0002 NP per day from November 1991 to October 1992, and by 0.0004 per day from then till 19 December 1994.
Source: Banco de México.

31

significant adjustment of policies to defend the existing exchange-rate system. The need for adjustment was also reinforced by monetary tightening in the United States. For much of the period from mid-March onwards, the peso came under downward pressure and remained close to the bottom of the fluctuation band.

Faced with these pressures on the currency, the main monetary policy and exchange-rate options available to the Mexican authorities were to:

- maintain the exchange-rate commitment, by tightening domestic monetary conditions or using the stock of international reserves, to the extent necessary to defend the exchange rate;
- increase the rate of depreciation of the exchange-rate band to try to engineer a gradual real depreciation;
- make a substantial once-off devaluation and re-peg;
- float the exchange-rate and establish an alternative nominal anchor (for example, an inflation target).

The first of these options might have been viewed as unduly restrictive, particularly given the background of disappointing growth and problems of asset quality in the banking system (discussed below), which monetary tightening could be expected to aggravate in the short term. On the other hand, it could be argued that the importance of any real over-valuation by 1994 was uncertain, and that the credibility of the government's exchange-rate commitment was an important policy asset that should not be discarded lightly. Moreover, each of the available policy options would probably also have had to be combined with some degree of domestic monetary tightening to ensure that any change of exchange-rate regime did not lead to a renewed inflationary spiral or loss of confidence in financial markets.

Against this background, monetary policy in 1994 does not appear with hindsight to have been strongly restrictive. Short-term interest rates were increased sharply after March, reversing falls that had taken place over the previous year, but it proved insufficient to rein in growth of the broad money and credit aggregates. A number of broad aggregates, including M3 and total credit outstanding, continued to grow at annual rates in the vicinity of 20 per cent throughout 1994 (Figure 11).[30] The central bank's net domestic credit (defined as the monetary base less official reserves) also expanded sharply, largely reflecting the bank's purchases of domestic securities to sterilise reserve losses after March 1994. Growth of the monetary base (mainly comprising notes and coin in

Figure 11. **MONETARY INDICATORS**

Annual percentage change

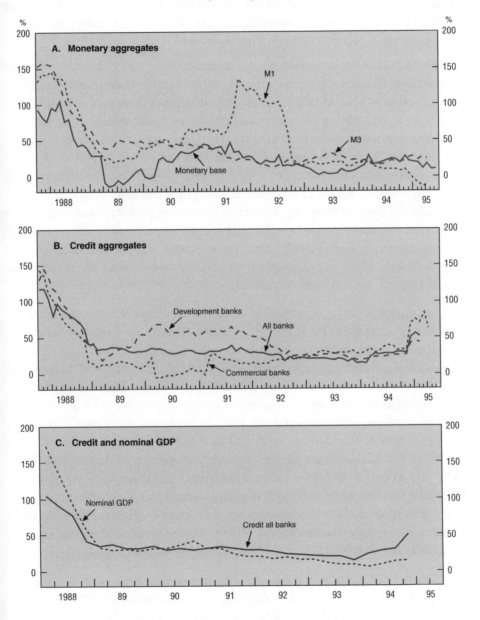

Source: Banco de México.

the hands of the public) accelerated to more than 20 per cent; at the same time M1 (comprising notes and coin and current deposits) grew at a lower rate than the monetary base and slowed substantially compared with 1993, reflecting reduced holdings of peso-denominated checking accounts.

The acceleration in growth of the monetary base in 1994 could be partly explained as accommodating an increase in demand for base money resulting from a number of special factors. These included the trend reduction of inflation, as well as a substitution from current deposits to cash, reflecting interest rate reductions and increases in bank charges which may have made current deposits less attractive. There was also a short-term effect in the early part of the year from capital inflows that were not fully sterilised. Nonetheless, in circumstances where important structural changes and shifts in financial asset composition were occurring, the broader monetary and credit aggregates probably provided a more representative picture of overall financial conditions, and these were generally showing relatively high growth rates. Bank interest margins declined slightly prior to March 1994, but subsequently increased in line with increases in the general level of interest rates (Figure 12).

An important factor contributing to overall credit growth was the acceleration of credit expansion by development banks (Table 11). As discussed above, this expansion was largely policy-driven, since the development banks benefit from *de facto* government backing in raising funds in the market and their overall credit growth is constrained mainly by ceilings set by the Ministry of Finance. These ceilings were raised progressively, allowing credit growth by development banks to accelerate in each year from 1991 to 1994, and the annual increase in their credit outstanding during that period to rise from around 1 to around 4 per cent of GDP.[31] A significant, though declining, proportion of development bank credit was extended to public sector institutions, including state governments. While development bank lending was partly intended to overcome market failures in providing credit to small borrowers, such rapid credit growth undoubtedly had an expansionary macroeconomic effect, which contributed to the growing current account deficit.

Growth of credit to the private sector by commercial banks was also rapid in recent years and was consistently faster than growth of nominal GDP, reflecting a combination of factors including easier access to credit following financial deregulation and privatisation of the commercial banks, improvements in the

34

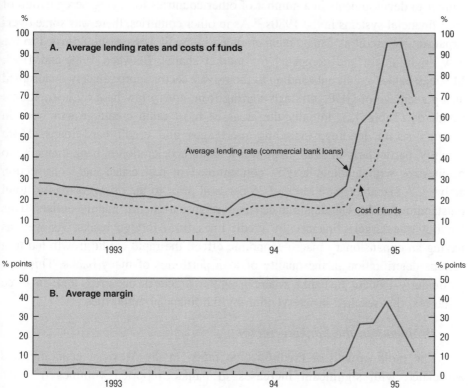

Figure 12. **BANK INTEREST MARGINS**

Per cent annual

A. **Average lending rates and costs of funds**

Average lending rate (commercial bank loans)

Cost of funds

B. **Average margin**

Source: Banco de México.

Table 11. **Credit growth by development banks**

Percentage changes unless otherwise indicated

	1991	1992	1993	1994[1]
Credit to the public sector	−0.5	11.1	7.0	22.0
(Per cent of total)	(58.3)	(51.5)	(42.9)	(38.9)
Credit to the private sector	42.9	46.0	51.4	41.8
Total credit	13.9	25.7	28.5	33.4
Increase in credit outstanding[2]	1.4	2.5	3.2	4.2[3]
Financial intermediation[2]				
(Public accounts definition)	1.2	1.1	2.9	3.6

1. November/November figure is used, to abstract from extraordinary effects on foreign currency loans of the December 1994 depreciation.
2. Per cent of nominal GDP.
3. Estimates.
Source: Banco de México.

35

government finances and capital inflows. In many respects this experience was similar to developments in a number of other countries following deregulation of their financial systems in the 1980s.[32] As in other countries, there was some over-expansion of credit as banks, inexperienced in credit assessment, adjusted to the new environment and competed for market shares. Between 1988 and 1994, Mexican banks' credit outstanding to the private sector approximately quadrupled as a percentage of GDP, although starting from a very low base by international standards (Table 12). Initially the areas of most rapid credit growth were in personal-sector lending, including mortgages and credit card loans. More recently, particularly in 1994, there was a major acceleration in bank financing to businesses, with lending heavily concentrated in real estate and construction activity. A sizeable share (around 25 per cent prior to the crisis) of banks' total outstanding credit was denominated in foreign currencies, mainly dollars. This lending was largely financed by credit lines from foreign banks. As well as having an expansionary macro-economic effect, the rapid credit growth led to a serious deterioration in the quality of loan portfolios of many banks. This was particularly evident in banks where irregular practices occurred, and, in three instances, this resulted in intervention by the financial authorities.

Problems in the banking sector

The rapid growth of credit/income ratios in the Mexican economy was associated with significant increases in banks' reported volumes of non-

Table 12. **Credit to the private sector**

Per cent of GDP, end year

	1988	1989	1990	1991	1992	1993	1994
Enterprises	9.9	13.2	15.8	18.9	22.9	26.0	35.5
Households	4.3	6.8	8.6	11.7	15.9	18.3	19.8
Total	14.2	20.0	24.4	30.6	38.8	44.3	55.3
Memorandum item: Foreign currency- denominated loans as per cent of total	25.1	19.2	20.2	22.6	18.5	20.5	27.1

Source: Banco de México.

performing loans (Table 13). These increased from 2.3 per cent of the aggregate loan portfolio in 1990 to 9.5 per cent by the end of 1994, with the overall level of recorded non-performing loans being slightly higher in the personal than in the business sector. These figures almost certainly understate the seriousness of the problem, due to a number of features of Mexican reporting standards which are less stringent than internationally accepted practices. In particular, and contrary to international practice, only the overdue portion of an unpaid obligation (rather than the full amount) is counted as non-performing, which is likely to lead to important reporting lags, although this effect is mitigated by the relatively short average maturity of loan portfolios and the fact that the overdue amounts have to be recorded more quickly than under international standards. Despite these reporting deficiencies, it was clear that problems of asset quality were serious by the end of 1994. Banks' loan-loss reserves, although rising, covered only around 50 per cent of the volume of non-performing loans, and the latter reached a level close to 100 per cent of the capital of the commercial banking system. In 1994, loan-loss provisions began to have a major impact on bank profitability, and aggregate profits of the commercial banks turned negative in the second half of the year. Therefore, even before the impact of the exchange-rate crisis, the

Table 13. **Banking sector balance sheet indicators**

Per cent

	1990	1991	1992	1993	1994	March 1995
Non-performing loans/total loans	2.0	3.1	5.7	7.4	7.4	9.8
Non-performing consumption loans/ total consumption loans	5.9	5.0	10.7	15.1	19.0	22.2
Non-performing housing loans/ total housing loans	0.8	0.6	2.5	4.0	5.5	5.5
Loan-loss reserves/non-performing loans	10.7	35.6	48.3	42.7	48.3	55.4
Loan-loss reserves/total loans	0.2	1.1	2.7	3.2	3.6	5.4
Net profit/total revenues	4.4	5.0	6.5	7.1	2.7	1.9
Non-performing loans *minus* loan-loss reserves/capital	17.7	22.6	34.0	47.2	49.9	52.3

Source: CNBV.

37

banking system was already facing serious adjustment problems, and a significant part of credit growth may have begun to reflect capitalisation of interest on loans. Supervisory authorities were aware of this practice and, in the last quarter of 1994, requested the banks to abandon it so as to make increased provisions. These requirements were formalised in January 1995.

Policy response to the growing exchange-rate pressures

The combination of financial developments outlined above meant that the authorities were faced with a variety of conflicting pressures when formulating monetary policy. Downward pressure on the exchange rate and credit expansion suggested a need for tightening, but real interest rates were already relatively high, and the vulnerability of the banking system and uncertain state of the economic recovery were felt by the central bank to limit the scope for interest rate increases.[33] Against this background, the authorities adopted a strategy for defending the exchange rate which did not rely exclusively on monetary tightening. The main elements of the strategy were: a significant increase in short-term interest rates (by around 8 percentage points) following the initial shock in March; depreciation of the peso within the fluctuation band (which allowed an immediate depreciation of about 10 per cent), with heavy intervention in support of the peso at its lower limit; and replacement of a large volume of conventional short-term government paper by Tesobonos (dollar-indexed securities) as a means of retaining the funds of investors who feared devaluation (see Figure 13). From mid-March onwards, the exchange rate remained close to the bottom of the band except for a few brief periods.

Although the initial interest rate increase in March was fairly substantial, its effect was partly eroded as rates were allowed to fall over the remainder of the year while short-term interest rates in the United States were rising. The interest differential on 3-month Treasury securities *vis-à-vis* the United States rose to a peak of around 12 percentage points in April, gradually declining to around 8 percentage points by early December. At the same time there were substantial portfolio flows out of pesos into US dollars or dollar-linked assets. Foreign exchange reserves declined by around US$20 billion between mid-March and early December, with the losses largely concentrated in the periods following the Colosio assassination in March and other political disturbances in June and November. The equivalent of a further US$15 billion shifted from holdings of

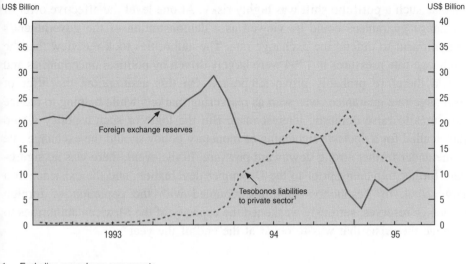

Figure 13. **FOREIGN RESERVES AND TESOBONOS LIABILITIES**

Foreign exchange reserves

Tesobonos liabilities
to private sector[1]

1. Excluding repurchase agreements.
Source: Banco de México.

Cetes (conventional short-term Treasury securities) into Tesobonos over the same period. By August, the value of Tesobonos liabilities of the Mexican government exceeded foreign exchange reserves and, although these portfolio flows stabilised over the subsequent three months, the renewal of outflows in November and December following further political disturbances quickly rendered the policy strategy unsustainable.

Both domestic and foreign investors appear to have been active in moving out of peso assets during 1994. Parts of the domestic corporate sector were heavily over-exposed to foreign-currency liabilities, mainly owed to domestic banks; this form of borrowing had been viewed as an attractive means to mini-mise interest costs. As confidence in the exchange rate deteriorated during 1994, a number of businesses sought to cover their exposures by building up offsetting foreign balances. Domestic residents were also active in switching to Tesobonos, often through domestic mutual fund holdings. However, around three-quarters of the overall switch into Tesobonos in the course of the year was accounted for by foreign investors, of which the most important group seems to have been US-based mutual funds specialising in emerging market securities.

In retrospect, the strategy of increasing Tesobonos supplies to help accommodate such a portfolio shift was highly risky. At one level the effective offer of exchange guarantees could be viewed as a demonstration of the government's commitment to defend the exchange rate. The authorities took the view that the exchange-rate pressures in 1994 were largely driven by political uncertainties and would therefore probably prove temporary. On this assumption, the offer of exchange-rate guarantees was seen as reassuring markets while helping to reduce pressures to raise domestic interest rates. But the logic of such a policy would have called for a decisive tightening of monetary policy should the exchange rate come under further strong downward pressure. In the event, there was no significant further tightening prior to the December devaluation, and the existence of a large stock of Tesobonos liabilities, coupled with the depletion of foreign exchange reserves, seriously weakened the capacity of the Mexican authorities to manage the crisis that was to occur at the end of the year.

The December crisis

In December, investors' worries about political stability and economic prospects in Mexico intensified. The current account deficit had risen rapidly. At the beginning of the month, news that the situation in Chiapas was worsening triggered a new wave of capital outflows. The renewed pressures against the peso were resisted mainly through sterilised intervention. There was no further tightening of domestic monetary policy and a relatively small further increase in Tesobonos supplies. Reserve losses accelerated, and by mid-December they were down to US$11 billion, compared with a peak of almost US$30 billion in February.

On 20 December, with the rate of reserve losses clearly unsustainable, the government widened the exchange-rate band, allowing the peso to devalue by 15 per cent – a move that was negotiated and agreed within the Pacto framework. The announcement shattered market confidence and, after a further US$5 billion in reserves were lost in defending the new floor, the exchange rate was allowed to float freely on 22 December. By the end of December, the peso had fallen by around 30 per cent from end-November – in addition to the 10 per cent depreciation within its band recorded since the start of the year. The downward move continued in January 1995. As the peso fell, interest rates increased sharply, the stock market crashed by over 40 per cent (though still only back to around its level of early 1993), and Mexican bond prices dropped on international markets (Figure 14).

When the exchange-rate band was widened, the market's reaction was particularly severe, reflecting a combination of factors. The devaluation represented the abandonment of a long-standing commitment which had been a centrepiece of the previous administration's policy strategy, and the delay before a convincing policy strategy could be put in place exacerbated the climate of uncertainty. In this environment, markets quickly came to the view that the 15 per cent devaluation was too small. In addition, foreign investors felt that there was insufficient communication when the decision to devalue was announced. The devaluation and the stabilisation package that followed were decided after negotiations in the Pacto, a valuable framework in the eyes of the authorities. But this process may have contributed to delaying decision-making.

In this climate, the stabilisation plan of 4 January, that included fiscal stringency and strict wage guidelines as well as a tight monetary policy framework, failed to reassure markets. The announcement in mid-January of an international financial support package consisting of up to US$18 billion credit, provided by governments, central banks, the BIS and commercial banks, soon followed by an IMF standby agreement (providing US$7.5 billion credit), also proved insufficient to restore confidence and stabilise markets. As the crisis unfolded in January and February, confidence deteriorated further as second round effects of the depreciation came into play. The fall in the exchange rate, which fluctuated around 6-7 pesos/dollar (a 40-50 per cent depreciation from pre-crisis levels), led to a reassessment of the repayment capacity of both public and private Mexican debtors. The two main sources of concern were the fragility of the banking sector, which quickly appeared to reach a critical point, and the government's capacity to repay dollar-indexed securities (Tesobonos).

Although the activities of individual classes of foreign investors are not well documented, anecdotal reports suggest that a number of large institutional holders of Tesobonos (mainly US-based mutual funds) sought to withdraw rapidly from the Mexican market, almost regardless of the exit price, in the wake of the devaluation announcement. Tesobonos holders were, in principle, protected against foreign exchange risk, but there was a perception that the design of these securities left them subject to a "conversion risk"; there were also reported fears

41

Figure 14. **FINANCIAL MARKET INDICATORS**

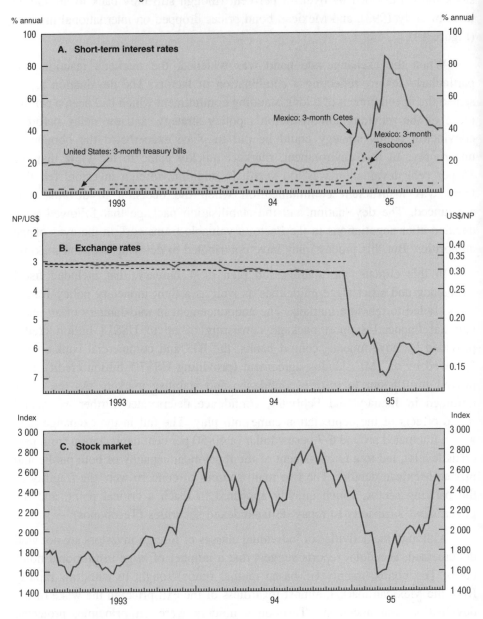

1. Auctions suspended after 15 February 1995.
Source: OECD, Banco de México and Datastream.

of a partial default on Tesobonos, either through imposition of capital controls to limit convertibility or through compulsory roll-overs.[34] Foreign investors had experienced such convertibility problems during the 1982 crisis. To some extent, these fears were self-reinforcing because they contributed to heavy selling pressures and a collapse of liquidity in the Tesobonos market, which made it extremely difficult for the government to refinance the maturing stock.

The depreciation of the peso, further rises in interest rates (to over 60 per cent by the end of February) and the worsening situation in the real economy also put pressure on the corporate sector and Mexican banks. Borrowers' capacity to service outstanding obligations deteriorated quickly. The reduced capacity of firms to service debt, in turn, added to the difficulties of commercial banks – already fragile before the currency crisis because of their high credit risk exposures. Although the full effect of the exchange-market crisis would take time to unfold, it became clear that to avoid a wider crisis of the financial system, special attention would need to be given to the banking sector (for details, see Part II below).

A case can be made in hindsight that markets over-reacted to the devaluation announcement and that investors' fears were exaggerated. The solvency of the Mexican government was not in doubt and there has been no default on Tesobonos liabilities. A number of Tesobonos holders realised losses unnecessarily by selling their holdings at heavy discounts. In a number of respects, Mexico's underlying situation at the end of 1994 was very different from that of 1982, at the time of the debt crisis. A primary budget surplus had replaced the considerable deficit of 1982 and public sector finances were close to balance overall. The size of the public enterprise sector had been reduced, which helped to restore fiscal discipline and improve efficiency. By 1994 manufactured products accounted for a major share of exports, whereas oil had previously been predominant. More generally, the economy, which had previously been very inward-oriented, was now open to trade, in particular because of NAFTA.

Despite this record of policy achievement over the previous twelve years, it has taken considerable time before a degree of confidence could be restored following the December crisis. Key factors in beginning to rebuild financial confidence were the announcement of an enhanced package of international liquidity support by President Clinton, and the subsequent strengthening of the Mexican government's stabilisation programme. The main elements of the international support programme announced at the end of January were US$20 billion in liquidity support from the United States and a total IMF standby facility of US$17.8 billion. At the beginning of March, the Mexican authorities announced a second package of measures to reinforce the January programme, reflecting the worse-than-expected developments in the early months of the year.

No single factor can explain the severity and timing of the December 1994 crisis, and it is important to distinguish between the underlying sources of pressure leading to the crisis and the more immediate factors that triggered and amplified it. The underlying pressures arose from an increasing incompatibility between the exchange-rate policy, under which the exchange-rate commitment had been used over a long period as a tool for disinflation, and some other aspects of macroeconomic policy which became more expansionary during 1993 and 1994. This combination, together with strong capital inflows, led to an upward trend in the real exchange rate over recent years and an unsustainable widening of the current account deficit. Important aspects of the shift in macro-economic policy stance were the relaxation of fiscal policy and rapid increase in development banks' financial intermediation. In addition, the adjustment to der-egulation of the domestic financial system fuelled overall credit growth as well as contributing to the emergence of balance-sheet problems that made the central bank reluctant to tighten policy as much as necessary to defend the exchange-rate policy. These pressures accumulated gradually over a period of time, and their impact on the foreign exchange market was to some extent obscured by highly volatile capital flows, with strong inflows stimulated by NAFTA ratification and subsequent outflows triggered by adverse political shocks.

Even without these volatile triggering factors, the accumulation of pressures would probably at some stage have necessitated a significant policy adjustment. The two polar options available to the Mexican authorities as exchange-rate pressures developed during 1994 were to change the exchange-rate regime allowing a major depreciation, or to tighten macroeconomic policies to defend the existing exchange-rate commitment. The authorities chose a middle course of avoiding major policy adjustments, while largely accommodating capital out-flows and flows into dollar-indexed securities. This resulted in a serious deterio-ration of the authorities' international liquidity position without removing the fundamental sources of pressure. From this perspective it seems likely that the adjustment imposed by financial markets through the December crisis was more severe than would have been necessary had timely policy action been taken.

II. Policy requirements in the short term

Following the collapse of confidence in the peso, the Mexican authorities adopted in January 1995 an economic emergency programme agreed with social partners. Additional measures were announced on 9 March, in response to continued volatility on the foreign exchange and financial markets. In the short term, the objective of the stabilisation programme is to reduce the current account deficit while preventing the development of a price-wage spiral. Structural reform measures are included in the programme, as well as special schemes designed to address the growing difficulties of the banking sector. At the end of January, in order to help stabilise financial and foreign exchange markets, international financial institutions and the United States government put together a package providing loans and loan guarantees to Mexico.

The policy response stands in sharp contrast to the 1982 debt crisis episode. Then, the immediate response following the collapse of the exchange market was to suspend payments on foreign debt, impose exchange controls (later followed by a dual exchange rate system), nationalise banks and impose permit requirements on all imports. This time, the government announced that structural reforms would not be postponed (they may even be accelerated in the case of privatisation); the liberalisation of trade and capital flows has been maintained; and a futures market has been created to allow covering of exchange rate risk. This part reviews the major planks of the government's strategy in the short term, focusing on the role of fiscal and monetary policy. Other supportive actions, such as the banking sector scheme and the international initiatives to address the liquidity problems, are then reviewed. Mexico's short-term economic prospects are discussed in the last section.

The economic emergency programme

Social concertation

The January stabilisation programme was agreed to by all social partners, within the Pacto framework. The new agreement, which replaced the initial Social Pact for 1995, signed in September 1994, was based on the assumption that the exchange rate of the peso would average 4.50 NP/$ in 1995 (although allowing for larger-than-usual volatility). Administered prices were increased by 10 per cent. Inflation over the twelve months to December was projected to be 19 per cent, while entrepreneurs agreed to limit price rises to adjustments induced by higher costs of imported inputs.[35] Minimum wages were raised by 7 per cent to cover the year, which implied a substantial fall in real terms. Workers earning less than twice the minimum wage would get an additional 3 per cent increase in income through a negative income tax.

By contrast, in March, the government announced the second package of measures outside of the Pacto framework, along with significant revisions to the official macroeconomic projections. GDP was projected to decline by 2 per cent (instead of the small increase projected in January); the exchange rate was assumed to average 6 NP/$ over the year; and the inflation projection was revised upwards to 42 per cent, December on December. A 12 per cent rise in minimum wage was to be granted on 1 April (to coincide with the increase in the VAT rate), while prices and wages were to be set freely. The negative income tax, provided for in the January Pacto, was extended to cover workers earning up to four times the minimum wage.

Fiscal policy

The initial budget for 1995, approved in early December 1994 just before the crisis, projected an overall budget balance based on a GDP growth forecast of 4 per cent. At 2.2 per cent of GDP, the primary surplus was to remain virtually unchanged from the 1994 outturn. This budget did not imply any fiscal tightening, despite the clear evidence that financial markets were concerned about developments in Mexico. It therefore did little to dispel the growing disquiet among international investors or to relieve pressures on the peso. The revised budget included in the January emergency package projected a primary surplus of

3.4 per cent of GDP, an increase of 1.2 percentage points from the initial budget, to be achieved through cuts on both current and capital expenditure.[36]

The reinforced March package provided for a further tightening of fiscal policy: the primary surplus was projected to rise to 4.4 per cent of GDP, through additional measures affecting both revenues and expenditure (Table 14). On the revenue side, the VAT rate was increased from 10 to 15 per cent on 1 April; public-sector energy prices were again raised (petrol by 35 per cent and electricity by 20 per cent). On the expenditure side, programmable spending is expected to be cut by nearly 10 per cent in real terms, through departmental rationalisation, staff reductions, hiring freezes and postponement of new infrastructure projects. A small surplus (0.5 per cent of GDP) is projected for the overall budget position, unchanged from the January programme, as the increase in the primary surplus offsets the expected rise in interest payments.

The government has reaffirmed that social spending would be preserved to the extent possible. Infrastructure investment is being delayed but current expenditures for basic education, health and other social programmes are to be maintained. Specific measures have been designed with the objective of protecting the poor from the heaviest burden of the adjustment, including:

– an increase in the number of training scholarships to serve as a sort of safety net in the absence of unemployment benefits: instead of 500 000 scholarships originally budgeted, 700 000 will be provided in 1995, half of them to unemployed workers,[37] and the rest to active workers, mostly employed in micro and small size enterprises;
– expansion of direct support for agriculture and livestock activities through PROCAMPO;[38]
– allocation of additional public funds to create 600 000 temporary jobs in particularly depressed areas.

The fiscal results for the first half of 1995 are on target although the outturn for the year remains subject to some uncertainty. The additional revenue to be generated by the newly-adopted policy measures will be highly dependent on the severity of the economic downturn, which may turn out to be deeper than projected. On the spending side, most of the required short-run savings may be obtained by a decline in public-sector real wages, while projected staff reductions and rationalisation of public administration are unlikely to yield results in the immediate future.

Table 14. Government budget for 1995: original and revised

Per cent of GDP

	1994	1995		
	Outturn	Original budget (Dec. 1994)	Stabilisation plan	
			Revised (Jan. 1995)	Reinforced (Mar. 1995)
Public sector				
Revenue	25.2	24.9	24.7	25.6
Federal government	16.8	16.7	16.8	17.3
Public enterprises[1]	8.5	8.2	7.9	8.3
Expenditure	25.6	24.9	24.2	25.1
Federal government[1]	16.2	15.6	15.4	–
Public enterprises[1]	9.4	9.3	8.7	–
Budgetary balance[2]	–0.3	0.0	0.6	0.5
Federal government				
Revenue				
Income tax	5.6	5.7	5.5	4.7
VAT	3.1	2.9	2.9	4.3
Excise taxes	2.2	2.2	1.7	1.7
Import duties	1.0	1.0	1.1	1.0
Other taxes	0.7	0.7	0.7	0.7
Non-tax revenue	4.2	4.2	5.0	4.9
Expenditure				
Wages and salaries	2.2	2.5	2.3	–
Goods and services	1.1	1.6	1.5	–
Interest payments	2.1	1.8	2.3	–
Current transfers[3]	6.1	4.8	4.7	–
Revenue sharing	3.3	3.2	3.2	–
Capital investment	1.3	1.4	1.2	–
Capital transfers	0.9	0.9	1.0	–
Public enterprises under budgetary control				
Budgetary revenue				
PEMEX	2.4	2.4	2.5	3.0
Public enterprises (excluding PEMEX)	6.0	5.8	5.5	5.2
Transfers	1.4	1.3	1.2	–
Budgetary expenditure				
Wages and salaries	2.6	2.6	2.5	–
Interest payments	0.4	0.4	0.5	–
Goods and services	4.4	4.3	n.a.	–
Capital expenditure	1.9	2.0	1.7	–

1. Net of transfers and interest payments between federal government and public enterprises.
2. Includes accounting differences from financing sources and non-budgetary controlled agencies.
3. Including transfers to public enterprises under budgetary control.
Source: Ministry of Finance.

Debt management in 1995 is oriented towards two key objectives: reducing the stock of outstanding Tesobonos and extending the average maturity of debt.

The stock of Tesobonos, including repurchase agreements (which were particularly high at the end of 1994), has been reduced from US$29 billion at the end of December 1994 to US$8.9 billion by mid July 1995. However, around US$7 billion of this reduction represented the unwinding of the repurchase arrangements, which have now returned to more usual levels. Most of the remaining reduction reflects the application of the international financial support package, which has enabled the government to replace some maturing Tesobonos with borrowings from the US government and the IMF.[39] The average maturity of total Mexican debt will tend to lengthen as a result of the new borrowing arrangements.

With the high interest rates that have prevailed since early 1995, several states and municipalities find themselves in a difficult financial position because the cost of debt servicing rose sharply. According to official analyses, 12 of the 31 states are facing particularly serious problems as most of the debt raised by state governments has been short-term loans from commercial banks. To address this situation, the government announced in early May a scheme designed to restructure debts associated with productive public work projects (previously registered with the Ministry of Finance). The voluntary scheme, amounting to NP 17.4 billion, equivalent to about 1 per cent of GDP, should help states and municipalities to restructure their debt, by converting it into long-term indexed securities, denominated in *Unidades de Inversión* (UDIs), *i.e.* units of account with a constant real value.[40]

Monetary policy

The main priorities of monetary policy in the aftermath of the crisis have been to:
- restore stability to the foreign-exchange market;
- maintain tight control over the growth of central bank domestic credit; and
- increase transparency of the central bank's operations in order to promote market confidence.

These objectives are interrelated and, in particular, stability in the foreign exchange market will hinge crucially on the extent to which markets are convinced that a sound monetary framework is in place.

The main monetary and financial policy commitments announced in the January package were a ceiling of NP 12 billion on central bank domestic credit creation, the elimination of further central bank credit to development banks and official trust funds, and a substantial reduction in the ceiling on development banks' financial intermediation to 2.1 per cent of GDP in 1995. The purpose of these commitments was to place limits on the capacity of government financial institutions to accommodate higher inflation in the post-crisis period. In particular, the ceiling on central bank domestic credit (defined essentially as the monetary base minus foreign exchange reserves)[41] would imply a limit on the Bank of Mexico's ability to expand the monetary base by providing credit to the government or by purchasing domestic securities. The ceiling was initially set to be sufficient to finance an increase in the monetary base of up to 21 per cent in 1995, approximately equivalent to the then-prevailing projection for nominal GDP growth. The ceiling was subsequently tightened despite a substantial upward revision to projected inflation.

Room for manœuvre in the conduct of monetary policy during the early months of 1995 proved to be very limited. With foreign reserves extremely low, there was little scope for official intervention to stabilise the peso. Monetary operations were mainly driven by the need to roll over short-term government paper, consistent with the cap on central bank domestic credit. Interest rates on Cetes set at weekly auctions reflected market assessments as to the risk of further currency depreciation. In the first quarter of 1995, with the peso/dollar exchange rate highly volatile around a depreciating trend, 3-month Cetes rates rose dramatically, peaking at over 80 per cent. Such rates reflected the considerable uncertainties that prevailed as markets assessed the overall stance of policy and the uncertain prospects about where the exchange rate might settle. Financial markets were highly illiquid, as institutions were reluctant to act as market makers in the volatile conditions.

Against this background the monetary policy commitments announced in January were strengthened in the March package, which included a tighter limit of NP 10 billion on central bank domestic credit, along with a number of measures to tighten control over liquidity to commercial banks. Markets became more stable from around this period, reflecting better understanding of the policy environment as well as the effect of the international support programme on confidence in the government's liquidity position. The exchange rate strengthened somewhat and then steadied around 6 NP/$ (the rate was 6.27 NP/$ at the end of June); short-term interest rates began to fall from their mid-March peaks of over 80 per cent, reaching around 40 per cent by the end of June. There was also some return of confidence in the Mexican stock market, which during March and April recovered around a third of the cumulative losses since the September 1994 peak and by mid-July was above its level at the start of 1995. To help promote liquidity in the foreign exchange market the government encouraged the establishment of a peso futures contract on the Chicago Mercantile Exchange, which began trading in April. The Bank of Mexico is also encouraging development of a domestic forward market.

The role of the net domestic credit ceiling in the overall policy strategy has been a subject of some debate among market observers. A number of technical criticisms have been raised and, as discussed below in Part III, the net domestic credit ceiling does not seem well suited to serve as a longer-run basis for monetary policy as the focus moves beyond crisis management. Nonetheless, in the immediate post-crisis period the ceiling has probably provided a useful safeguard against inflationary central bank financing and helped to reassure markets that the government's maturing domestic debts would not be monetised.

An important theme of policy debate in the post-crisis period has been the need for greater transparency in monetary policy. One aspect of policy transparency concerns the provision of information about the details of monetary operations. A criticism of previous practices was that foreign exchange reserves data were only disclosed with a considerable lag and that markets did not have sufficient information to monitor key aspects of central bank operations. In response to this criticism, in March 1995 the Bank of Mexico began publishing weekly balance sheet summaries including key variables such as the monetary base, foreign exchange reserves, net domestic credit and international borrowings. It is now committed to publishing this information with a maximum reporting lag of 3 working days. The bank has also announced that it is working to shorten to under two weeks publication lags of key variables reported in its monetary statistics and has moved to daily reporting of its monetary operations. In combination with improvements in fiscal disclosure (including a move to publication of monthly fiscal accounts), these measures should allay market concerns about policy transparency at the operational level. At a broader level, however, much remains to be done in providing information about the analytical framework guiding monetary policy decisions. These issues are taken up in Part III.

Measures of structural reform

The emergency programme includes measures of structural reform which, to a large degree, are a continuation and in some cases an acceleration of reforms that were already envisaged rather than new initiatives: telecommunication services (privatised in 1990) will be opened progressively to competition; and privatisation of ports, airports and railways will be accelerated. The Mexican government also plans to privatise some petrochemical plants and the Federal Electricity Commission is to sell securities backed by expected revenues from power plants. Revenue from the privatisation programme is likely to be low this year because of the delays involved in preparing the divestiture (for details on privatisation and deregulation, see Part IV). Ceilings on foreign investment in existing financial institutions were also partially lifted. The privatisation project of the new government is an important element of the programme because, besides being a source of revenue, it is a signal that the government is continuing along the reform strategy of the previous administration, which should contribute to strengthening financial market confidence.

Measures to assist the banking sector

The problems of balance-sheet quality that developed in Mexican banks over the period from 1988 to 1994 have been seriously compounded by the effects of the peso devaluation and interest-rate increases. The earlier problems were partly due to some bank managers' inexperience in operating in the deregulated environment, a phenomenon that occurred in several other OECD countries following financial deregulation; but they also reflected deficiencies in the prudential supervisory system (currently being addressed through a series of reforms that began in 1994).[42] Banks will be affected by the currency crisis through three main channels.[43] First, a significant proportion of commercial bank lending to domestic borrowers (around 22 per cent prior to the devaluation, rising to 30 per cent at the end of 1994 due to the devaluation effect) was denominated in foreign currencies; this is approximately matched on banks' balance sheets by foreign-currency-denominated liabilities, mainly to foreign banks. The exchange-rate depreciation could impair the repayment capacity of banks' foreign-currency borrowers, since, as outlined below, some of these borrowers' positions seem to have been unhedged.[44] Second, high interest rates that have followed the crisis (well over 80 per cent in the interbank market in March and April and around 45 per cent by mid-year) can be expected to have a major effect on borrowers' ability to repay, particularly in a context where many borrowers were already overcommitted and the economy is moving into recession. Deterioration of the loan portfolio has affected provision requirements and capitalisation, prompting the introduction of the temporary capitalisation programme described below. In addition, some borrowers stopped servicing their foreign currency debts in anticipation of an exchange-rate recovery or some form of government relief. Third, by inflating the peso value of banks' nominal balance sheets, exchange-rate depreciation reduced bank capital ratios by around one percentage point, although in aggregate they did not fall below official requirements. The full effect of these forces will take some time to become apparent. Available data for the first quarter of 1995 suggest a major increase in the volume of non-performing loans, although this is being partially offset by the debt restructuring programmes already implemented.

An important factor determining the overall impact of the crisis on the quality of banks' loan portfolios will be the financial exposures of the Mexican corporate sector, some indicators of which are summarised in Table 15. The sample of large companies included in the table appears to have been heavily exposed to foreign exchange risk. This results from earlier decisions to borrow in foreign currencies as a means of minimising interest costs, based on expectations that the risk of a major depreciation was small. In many cases, exposures to foreign-currency denominated debt exceeded the natural hedge provided by foreign earnings. Devaluation could therefore have a significant effect on cash flows of the affected companies, although this will be mitigated by the loan restructuring programmes outlined below. Higher interest rates on peso-denominated borrowings could also have a severe short-term impact on the corporate sector's profitability and hence on its capacity to service debt, although this too will depend importantly on the success of the loan restructuring schemes currently being implemented.

In response to the developing problems of loan portfolio quality, the supervisory authorities moved in early 1995 to tighten prudential standards and increase provision requirements in the banking system. In addition, there were a

Table 15. **Corporate sector: financial indicators** [1]

NP billion, unless otherwise specified

	Samples of 59 companies	Ten largest
Total sales	219.1	117.4
(Per cent foreign)	(9.0)	(7.9)
Total liabilities	152.8	72.8
(Per cent denominated in foreign currency)	(59.1)	(61.7)
Gross profits	34.4	20.5
(As per cent of assets)	(9.7)	(11.4)
Debt/equity ratio	0.76	0.67
Memorandum item:		
Mexican banks' foreign currency loans to non-financial private sector, December 1994	179.4	

1. Mexican stock-exchange statistics for listed industrial and commercial companies, latest available 12-month reporting period for each company as at March 1995.
Source: OECD calculations based on Stock Exchange data.

series of special measures aimed at easing the current financial pressures on the banking system, details of which are set out in the accompanying Box. The main components of these measures are:

- a dollar liquidity window provided by the Bank of Mexico to help banks to refinance maturing short-term foreign credit lines;
- a temporary capitalisation programme, under which a special trust fund (PROCAPTE) will inject additional capital into the banking system in the form of mandatory convertible debentures over a five-year period;
- easing of equity restrictions to help attract new capital into the banking sector;
- a set of loan restructuring programmes under which the government facilitates the converting of a proportion of banks' outstanding loans into inflation-indexed form, so as to reduce the immediate payment burdens on borrowers; and
- improvement of the banks' capitalisation levels by transactions exchanging a portion of their loan portfolios net of provisions for government bonds, conditional on the banks raising new capital.

Details of bank assistance measures

The bank assistance measures announced early in 1995 consisted of the following main components.

Dollar liquidity mechanism. The Bank of Mexico is providing a special dollar credit window to Mexican banks, at a penalty interest rate, to help ease liquidity pressures arising from required repayments of their foreign debts. Around three-quarters of the foreign debt of Mexican banks is of short maturity (less than one year) and the banks faced serious difficulties in rolling over these debts in the early months of the financial crisis. Use of the scheme was initially substantial, with the total amount outstanding peaking at $3.8 billion in early April before declining to $1.5 billion by the end of June. The scheme is funded using part of the resources made available under the international support programme.

Temporary capitalisation programme. A special trust fund (PROCAPTE) has been set up to inject capital into the banking system in the form of mandatory convertible subordinated debentures. The programme is funded by borrowing from the central bank, with the monetary impact fully offset by a system of compensating reserve deposits. Banks which are currently capitalised below the 8 per cent requirement can obtain capital from PROCAPTE for a period of up to five years, after which amounts not repaid will be converted to ordinary capital and sold by the government. Earlier conversion can also take place at the initiative of the government in cases where capitalisation falls significantly below the programme average or where Tier 1 capital falls below 2 per cent at any time within the five year period. The scheme is aimed at supporting institutions rather than shareholders, and is not intended as a means for dealing with insolvencies, which will continue to be the responsibility of FOBAPROA, the existing agency for assisting insolvent banks. By mid-July six institutions had accessed PROCAPTE funding.

Easing of equity restrictions in banking. A number of restrictions on equity participation in the Mexican banking system have been eased. These measures are aimed at attracting foreign and corporate equity to help re-capitalise troubled institutions, particularly by NAFTA-country banks which may be interested in establishing networks in Mexico. Foreign acquisition of Mexican banks, previously prohibited entirely, will now be permitted by banks from other NAFTA countries for all but the three largest Mexican banks (a provision designed to ensure continued Mexican control of the payments system); these three banks together account for around half of the assets of the commercial banking system. Market-share limits on acquisition of Mexican credit institutions by NAFTA banks have been raised from 1.5 per cent to 6 per cent for individual banks, and from 6 per cent to 25 per cent in the aggregate. In addition, the general limit on foreign ownership of shares in banks remaining in domestic hands will effectively rise from 30 to 49 per cent, and limits on shareholdings by Mexican corporations have also been eased. Finally, individual limits on stock ownership rise from 10 to 20 per cent.

Loan restructuring programmes. The government has announced a number of loan restructuring programmes totalling approximately NP 163 billion, equivalent to around 23 per cent of the aggregate loan portfolio of the commercial banks. The programmes target small- and medium-sized companies, mortgage loans, state and municipal govern-

(continued on next page)

(continued)

ments, development banks and foreign-currency-denominated loans. The restructuring programmes establish a CPI-indexed accounting unit known as the UDI, and provide for loans to be re-denominated in this unit. The government facilitates the transformation of loan payments from real to nominal terms to the banks. This result is achieved by permitting banks to transfer loans, up to the allocated quotas, to special trust funds which convert each loan to a long-term fixed-rate indexed loan (*i.e.* denominated in UDIs), bearing a real interest rate of 4 per cent plus a margin to reflect the credit risk of the borrower. The Mexican government effectively accepts a claim on the net income of the trust funds, in return for which it issues floating rate bonds of equivalent expected value to the banks. These programmes are intended to ease cash flows of borrowers by facilitating a rescheduling of loan payments, but banks will explicitly retain responsibility for any credit risks on the restructured loans. However, the government bears the interest-rate risk inherent in the commitment to transform the interest payments to banks. This means eventually the government can incur losses to the extent that real interest rates turn out to be higher than assumed under the programme. The government is also encouraging the banks to make wider use of UDIs beyond these programmes by raising UDI deposits that can match further UDI-denominated loans. The banking institutions are also implementing their own restructuring programmes.

Additional mechanisms to capitalise banks. In two cases the Mexican government has participated in financial packages to facilitate the injection of fresh private capital. Key elements of the packages included: increases in loan provisions by the banks, effectively reducing the value of claims by existing shareholders; injection of new capital (through a foreign takeover in one case and through new capital raised from existing shareholders in the other); and the purchase by the government of a portion of the loan portfolio net of provisions, paying for it with government bonds. The financial authorities are analysing the possible extension of similar schemes to other institutions.

The new support programmes are intended to minimise the extent of probable government subsidies and are targeted at banks whose underlying positions are judged to be solvent. Funding through PROCAPTE will not be available to banks that do not have positive net worth, and the loan restructuring programmes explicitly exclude any transfer of credit risk from banks to government agencies. Provided these principles are maintained in practice, these programmes should not have major fiscal costs, and should be useful in providing a breathing space to banks that are solvent but under-capitalised. Bank insolvencies are to be handled outside the special programmes through FOBAPROA, the existing agency for dealing with bank insolvencies. The normal method for dealing with such cases would be for the agency to take over and refloat insolvent institutions at the best possible price. It cannot be ruled out that in some cases this may require substantial fiscal injections to restore such institutions to positive net worth. However, efforts to attract foreign equity capital into the banking sector could have an important role to play in containing these costs and, as discussed in Part IV, the Mexican banking sector could be viewed as an attractive investment prospect by foreign financial institutions.[45]

The net effects of the financial crisis and of the government's support programme on the Mexican private sector will take some time to unfold. The support programmes will provide partial relief from the contractionary forces arising from private-sector balance-sheet stress, but adjustment problems remain. For the non-financial private sector, gross losses on foreign-currency loans from Mexican banks were in some cases substantial, and interest rate increases on the scale seen in the first half of 1995 will have a major impact on cash flows of businesses and households. These effects will be partly mitigated by the officially sponsored debt restructuring schemes, which are limited to around 23 per cent of the volume of outstanding loans, while private sector cash flows will also be eased by additional restructuring programmes implemented by the banks. Exporting sectors can also be expected to benefit from substantially improved cash flows following the depreciation. However, as noted, the corporate sector in aggregate appears to have been over-exposed to foreign-denominated debts relative to the natural hedge provided by foreign earnings.

For the banking sector, it needs to be emphasised that the pre-crisis level of non-performing loans was already high relative to the banks' loan-loss reserves and relative to their capital base. Debt-repayment capacities of the household and corporate sectors will be impaired by the currency depreciation and high interest rates, making it likely that there will be further significant increases in loan losses. Moreover, low levels of current profitability will make it difficult for banks to rebuild their capital positions from internal resources. Nonetheless, legal reforms with respect to bank ownership, aimed at stimulating new capital injections, are already attracting fresh capital into the banking sector, which could prove an important factor in promoting recovery from current difficulties.

On the partial evidence available so far, the scale of these financial problems could be at least comparable to those experienced in a number of other countries where banking difficulties have recently been encountered, such as the United

States and a number of other English-speaking and Nordic countries.[46] The experience of these countries was that balance-sheet problems took considerable periods of time to resolve and had a major impact in deepening and prolonging recessions. Confidence generally took some time to be restored and the need for banks to rebuild their capital base often acted as a constraint on credit growth which tended to dampen economic recoveries. These experiences suggest that Mexico's problems of balance-sheet stress could be an important risk factor affecting near-term recovery prospects.

The financial rescue package

As the gale blowing through international financial markets in the aftermath of the December currency crisis was liable to put at risk the overall stability of emerging markets in Latin America and elsewhere, the need to help Mexico meet its immediate liquidity requirements became pressing. A multilateral financial rescue package was put together in January-February 1995, of which the main components are the following:

– US$20 billion to be provided by the United States, which could be short- or medium-term swap facilities having maturities from 3 months to 5 years, or long-term guarantees of securities having maturities of up to 10 years from the Treasury's Exchange Stabilisation Fund (ESF), or short-term swap facilities with maturities of up to one year from the Federal Reserve System. The first US$10 billion were provided in stages through 30 June; the second US$10 billion became available on 1 July. Provision of the funds is dependent on Mexico's implementation of economic policies agreed with the IMF;[47] all Mexico's obligations to the United States are guaranteed, in case of default, by proceeds of oil exports which are channelled through an escrow account at the Federal Reserve Bank of New York;

– SDR 12.1 billion (US$17.8 billion) in a 18-month standby arrangement from the International Monetary Fund, of which SDR 5.3 billion (US$7.75 billion) were paid immediately, while further disbursements are conditional upon the implementation of the economic adjustment programme.[48]

By the first week of July 1995, US$22.5 billion had been disbursed through these arrangements – of which US$12.5 billion came from the United States Treasury and the Federal Reserve, US$0.3 billion from the Bank of Canada and the rest from the IMF. Mexican authorities used these funds for three main purposes.[49] First, to redeem maturing dollar-indexed Tesobonos: by July the stock of Tesobonos held outside the central bank had come down to US$10 billion (from US$29 billion at end December). Second, part of the funds served to refinance commercial banks' foreign currency liabilities, such as external credit lines and foreign currency denominated CDs; at the end of June, about US$4.3 billion had been drawn for this purpose. Finally, funds have been used to strengthen foreign currency reserves, which at the end of June stood at about to US$10 billion.

The short-term outlook

Prospects are bleak for this year. By mid-May, the peso, at around 6NP/$, had fallen by 40 per cent compared to its pre-crisis level. Short-term interest rates, having dropped from a peak of 80 per cent in mid-March were still in a 50-60 per cent range, falling further thereafter, to 40 per cent at end-June. The impact of the depreciation of the peso and restrictive policies has started to show up.

Monthly consumer price inflation peaked at 8 per cent in April, with the impact of the VAT rise and public price adjustments compounding the effects from the depreciation.[50] Declining since then, monthly inflation reached 3.2 per cent in June – implying a 37.7 per cent rise from a year earlier. The decline of activity in the non-tradeable sector appears to have been quick and widespread. Construction output, for instance, fell by 13 per cent in the first quarter of 1995, compared with the same period a year earlier. According to official estimates, more than 750 000 job losses were recorded during the first quarter of the year. The open unemployment rate rose to 6.7 per cent in April, more than 3 percentage points above a year earlier.[51] The current account deficit narrowed to US$1.2 billion in the first quarter of 1995, from US$7 billion in the first quarter of 1994; in January-May, the trade account recorded a US$2.2 billion surplus instead of a deficit of US$7.2 billion a year earlier, including trade of in-bond industries. Merchandise exports in dollars rose by a record 33 per cent over a year earlier: those of maquiladoras increased by a more modest 20 per cent, in line with trends of recent years, while other manufacturing exports were up by 44 per cent. The quick response of the exporting sector is partly ascribable to improved price competitiveness. However, since prices for many goods are set in dollars (*i.e.* Mexico is a price-taker), the export boom is also largely the result of the reduction in domestic absorption, which has induced a shift of sales to foreign markets. Total imports in dollar terms decreased: imports of consumer and investment goods have fallen drastically, though those of intermediate products have remained strong.

Despite a substantial positive contribution to growth from the real foreign balance, GDP may decline by 3 to 4 per cent in 1995 as all components of domestic demand fall sharply (Table 16). The decline in output will be reflected in deteriorating labour market conditions, with employment in the formal sector of the economy as well as real wages falling significantly. Evidence over the first months of the year suggests that wage settlements have been very moderate.

Table 16. **Short-term projections**

Percentage changes from previous period

	1993	1994	1995	1996
Demand and output				
Private consumption	0.2	3.7	−8.0	1.0
Public consumption	2.0	2.5	−9.5	−1.0
Gross fixed investment	−1.2	8.1	−22.4	5.1
Final domestic demand	0.1	4.5	−11.3	1.6
Stockbuilding [1]	−0.3	0.0	−0.7	0.0
Total domestic demand	−0.3	4.5	−11.9	1.6
Exports of goods and services	3.7	7.3	18.0	10.0
Imports of goods and services	−1.3	12.9	−25.0	9.0
Foreign balance [1]	0.9	−0.9	8.3	1.1
GDP at market prices	0.7	3.5	−3.5	2.5
Prices				
GDP price deflator	10.0	7.4	28.0	24.0
Private consumption deflator	9.3	6.6	35.0	27.0
Current account balance [2]	−6.4	−7.7	−1.0	−1.0

1. As a percentage of GDP in the previous period.
2. As a percentage of GDP.
Source: OECD.

Wage projections are difficult to make since the minimum wage rise – announced by the government outside the Pacto framework in April this year – only serves as a reference in decentralised wage negotiations which also take into account productivity gains at the firm level. According to survey data, real earnings in manufacturing fell by 9 per cent in the first quarter of 1995 from a year earlier. Substantial real wage losses are likely to continue to be recorded during the second quarter of the year, as the deterioration of labour market conditions keep wage claims subdued, while price rises continue at very high rates before abating in the second half of the year. As informal activities expand, however, non-wage incomes will attenuate somewhat the fall of household disposable income and hence private consumption. Investment by Mexican firms may drop sharply in 1995 as a result of high interest rates, poor balance-sheet positions and the still uncertain business climate. Consumer prices may rise by 50 per cent over the 12 months to December 1995, with average inflation for the year of 35 per cent.

Improved price competitiveness should contribute to large gains in export markets. As import volumes fall, reflecting sharp cuts in consumer and investment demand, the improvement in the trade balance is likely to continue to be substantial over the coming months, so that the current account could reach near balance on average for 1995, as in the government's projections.

A rebound in activity can be expected from around the turn of the year. This outlook hinges crucially on two conditions. First, that investors' confidence, which appears to have strengthened since late March, is maintained over the coming months, so that interest rates come down progressively and the exchange rate remains close to 6 NP/$ on average, its early May level. Second, that a wage-price spiral does not develop, so that the real depreciation is preserved. Given the severe balance-sheet problems of the private sector, the pace of the recovery is likely to be slow and it will in part depend on the extent to which foreign direct investment increases to take advantage of lower prices and costs.

III. Towards a medium-term macroeconomic policy framework

Experience of other OECD countries has amply demonstrated the advantages of implementing policies within a coherent medium-term framework. While 1995 is bound to be a year of crisis management and adjustment for the Mexican economy, it would be necessary to put in place such a framework as soon as possible. This would help to anchor expectations and foster market confidence in government policy, thereby facilitating the ongoing adjustment. In compliance with the Constitution, the new government announced in May 1995 a strategy programme, the National Development Plan, providing general policy directions and overall projections for the six-year period that has just begun ("sexenio"). The usefulness of such a programme will be enhanced if it is followed by the introduction of a medium-term policy framework with a clear and credible statement of the principles that will guide policy making, backed up by projections and concrete plans. This chapter discusses some key elements and considerations pertinent to such a framework for macroeconomic policies, drawing on experience in other OECD countries.

Fiscal policy and public administration

Medium-term fiscal policy settings

The medium-term fiscal policy objective of the present administration is to return to budget balance (from the 1995 projected surplus) – a target that has the advantages of being readily understood and easily monitored (once definitions are agreed upon). In contrast to most other OECD countries,[52] Mexico has the hard-won advantages of having already achieved budget balance in the past and rapidly reduced its public debt to relatively low levels, so that maintaining budget balance over the medium term should be less difficult than in many other OECD countries from a public finances point of view. Nevertheless, certain factors may make the development of a sound and credible medium-term fiscal strategy more complicated than may first appear.

The current stabilisation programme requires very tight fiscal policy in the short term. For some time in the future, fiscal policy settings will need to take into account Mexico's reduced capacity to borrow on international financial markets, which implies that investment will need to be financed to a greater extent by domestic savings. Since international experience suggests that there is relatively little that government policy can do to influence the private savings rate, government savings will need to fill the gap.[53]

The transition from the current fiscal stance to a more neutral fiscal position over the medium term will need to be managed prudently and carefully, in order to avoid undermining overall macroeconomic objectives, even if this requires the government to maintain a fiscal surplus for some time rather than returning quickly to budget balance. The economic cycle will need to be taken into account in this transition. Although there are no estimates of structural budget balances, it is nevertheless clear that if overall budget balance is achieved in 1995 despite the fall in GDP, then the underlying structural budget balance (i.e. adjusted for the economic cycle) would be in surplus and current tax policy settings would be able to generate much stronger revenues as economic activity recovers. But meeting the objective of budget balance in the face of stronger cyclical revenues by preventing an *ex ante* surplus from being realised[54] would be procyclical and risk destabilising the economy. This argues for choosing a medium-term fiscal target that is flexible enough to take account of fluctuations in economic activity. Policy making in this regard would be facilitated by the development of measures of structural budget balances.[55] Notwithstanding the technical difficulties in developing estimates of structural budget balances in a country such as Mexico that has undergone widespread structural reforms, such a measure would help to improve fiscal management.[56]

Mexico's credibility has been damaged in international markets and special efforts will be needed to repair it. Despite Mexico's remarkable turnaround in fiscal performance in the late 1980s and early 1990s, demonstrating a prudent approach to fiscal policy in the future is likely to be an essential part of rebuilding credibility. Financial markets may demand that Mexico maintains a surplus for some time, especially given the increase in its outstanding debt as a per cent of GDP, due to the valuation effects of dollar-linked instruments. Credibility would be enhanced by the development of more concrete fiscal projections that would demonstrate the path to the medium-term objectives. Indeed Mexico is one of the few OECD countries that does not publish forward projections of the fiscal position beyond the current budget year.[57] First and foremost, most OECD countries have integrated forward projections into their budget planning process[58] as a way of improving the quality of their decision-making at the macroeconomic level – by indicating the fiscal position that would result from unchanged policy ("baseline" projections) – and at the structural level – by helping to identify how much different policy changes would contribute to closing the gap between the baseline and the desired fiscal position consistent with medium-term objectives. But if these forward projections are not published, financial markets are left to wonder about the future direction of fiscal policy and the medium-term consequences of current decisions. Publication of forward projections might not only inform and reassure markets directly but also provide an additional incentive for the government to stick to its chosen path, knowing that its credibility is at stake.

Some uncertainty remains about the government's contingent liabilities with respect to the banking sector and the budget's sensitivity to unanticipated exogenous changes, especially in interest rates and oil prices. The schemes to deal with weaknesses in the banking sector (discussed in Part II), are designed so that the taxpayer will not incur the cost, but the possibility cannot be ruled out that there will be some impact on the budget, even though the effect may be postponed until some time in the future. Likewise the future evolution of macroeconomic variables, especially those affecting the cost of debt servicing, are particularly uncertain at the present time and could place additional pressures on the budget. Any weakening of international oil prices would also affect the budget adversely. Other countries facing uncertainties related to the volatility of price movements in petroleum and mining sectors have chosen different strategies. In Norway, the question of institutionalising the accumulation of petroleum proceeds in a special fund has been under consideration since the early 1980s; finally, a Petroleum Fund was established in 1991, although it has remained empty due to political circumstances.[59] Chile, on the other hand, introduced the Copper Stabilisation Fund (CSF) in 1981, which forces the state to save a part or all of its extra income from copper exports during periods in which world prices exceed a reference price constructed according to historical information; the CSF has contributed substantially to domestic savings since the late 1980s, with receipts being used mainly for prepayment of government debt. In sum, the risks and uncertainty surrounding a number of fiscal variables would seem to be particularly large at present and this would also suggest that a particularly prudent approach should be taken in order to preserve room for manœuvre in the event of adverse developments.

Improving the effectiveness of public spending

Given these overall macroeconomic considerations, many programmes that require spending increases are being delayed and the main focus of the budget over the next few years is rather to improve the effectiveness of public spending and taxation. Considerable efforts have already been made in recent years to reorient public spending towards social development with special emphasis on alleviating extreme poverty. The Zedillo Administration intends to reinforce action in the areas of health, education and training as part of its strategy to break the poverty cycle. Specific policy measures and programmes are discussed in some depth in Part V.

Expansion in the areas of social development will have to be financed either through expenditure savings made elsewhere or through tax increases. Saving on expenditure may require reconsidering priorities and cutting some low-priority spending programmes. There also seems to be scope for savings to be made in the core administrative functions, both through organisational rationalisation and through raising public-sector productivity. A review of the functions of each government ministry to examine the scope for rationalisation of activities (both at the federal level and between the federal level and states and municipalities) is already under way. One step that would facilitate this rationalisation process would be to enhance the financial accounting and reporting systems to provide comparative costs of carrying out different functions. The Mexican government announced in the National Development Plan its intention to undertake an in-depth reform of both the present institutions and the internal and external public administration control mechanisms and to adopt the legal framework necessary to provide timely information to the public. The original budget documents for 1995 present detailed objectives and measures for each budget programme,[60] but their costs are not explicit, making "value for money" assessments very difficult.

Raising public-sector productivity will inevitably require some shedding of staff, and a programme of voluntary severance, providing several months' training to participants, has already been put into place. This programme is an important step in the right direction but may not lead to sufficient reductions in staffing levels. Experience in other countries also suggests that there is a risk of adverse selection, because the most valuable and productive civil servants are also those most easily employable elsewhere and therefore most willing to leave voluntarily.

More generally, the need to re-examine how the public service is managed has been recognised by the government. At present there are some 10 000 federal government positions that are filled through a political appointment process, in a system that is similar to the United States. Appointees to these positions are not covered by any specific law or regulation. They generally work in teams; when a minister or deputy minister moves, the whole team is likely to move. These appointees effectively make all policy and management decisions. The rest of the public-sector positions are characterised by low productivity and much lower pay. These workers' labour rights, job security in particular, are an integral part of the Constitution. While there are advantages in a political approach to public sector management – including a high degree of responsiveness to changes in political direction and a regular turnover of people – there are also weaknesses some of which became particularly apparent in the crisis. The transition period between administrations is relatively long – fourteen weeks – and it involves considerable upheaval since political appointments are extensive, creating a period where the capacity of government to function effectively is weak. Mexico was still undergoing this transition when the crisis erupted in December 1994 making a quick and effective response more difficult. Recognising the need to improve the present system, the Mexican government has announced its intention of developing a professional career in the civil service.

Taxation

Various tax reform measures were introduced at the end of the 1980s to increase the government's capacity to raise tax revenue, while reducing distortions and harmonising the Mexican system with those prevailing abroad.[61] Fur ther improvements are under study and a fiscal commission has been established to review the tax system with this objective, as well as to promote savings and investment. The Commission is examining simplification, compliance and the judicial framework governing interpretation of tax laws. Questions concerning the allocation of tax resources between the different levels of government will also be addressed, with a review of the existing redistribution formula and the scope for greater revenue raising at the state and municipal levels. The Commission has started to report its findings and this exercise should be completed by the end of 1995.

Debt management

The range of domestic government debt instruments of medium- and long-term maturity is relatively limited in Mexico, compared with several other OECD countries (see Annex I, Table A1). A recent survey of government debt management in OECD countries has identified a range of objectives that would form part of an effective debt management strategy, of which the following would seem to be most relevant for Mexico:[62]

- taking into account risks associated with different financing options in addition to the traditional objective of minimising debt servicing costs;
- achieving a balanced profile of maturing debt to avoid heavy bunching of maturing debt and thus minimise the market impact of government debt operations which could lead to erratic movements in prices and yields;
- broadening the range and distribution of government debt instruments, including an appropriate mix of short-, medium- and long-term maturities; and
- developing in particular longer-term instruments (including indexed instruments); in addition to facilitating the conduct of monetary policy by avoiding the problems of bunched conversions, this also provides valuable information to authorities about the term-structure of interest rates and inflation expectations.

In the light of these objectives, a medium-term objective for Mexico would be to put the emphasis on the development of a market for long-term government debt instruments, as and when it is able to do so while keeping debt servicing costs minimised. This would increase the government's room for manœuvre in response to adverse market conditions over the shorter run, as well as assist in the conduct of monetary policy.

Levels of government within the Federation

An important consideration in the context of medium term policy settings is the relationship between different levels of government. Mexico is a constitutional federation of 31 states (plus the Federal District of Mexico City) and more than 2 300 municipalities, characterised by highly centralised administration, with federal programmes accounting for most areas of government activity. Although the statistical base is not yet well developed, estimates indicate that in 1991 the federal government accounted for 78 per cent of total government expenditure. The share of state and local government employees in total public sector employment is one of the lowest among OECD countries, suggesting a relatively low degree of decentralisation (Table 17). Under the revenue sharing arrangements instituted in 1980, almost all taxes are collected by the federal government.[63] A part of these revenues is redistributed among the states and municipalities according to a formula based on a state's capacity to raise revenues directly and its population.

However, the activities carried out by the states and municipalities vary considerably and the division of functions between different levels has not always been systematic, leading to duplication of functions in some states and gaps in others. One channel through which federal funds have been disbursed to lower levels is the Solidarity programme (discussed in Part V) which provides a way of sharing the costs of development between the federal, states and municipal levels of government. In 1993, the federal government funding through Solidarity was equivalent to more than 50 per cent of total state expenditures. However, this programme was discretionary and some states seem to have been more effective at gaining a share of these federal resources than others. The distribution of federal resources (including Solidarity) for investment in 1990 shows that one third went to the federal district of Mexico City alone. Of the remainder, four states received more than twice the average per capita investment spending (excluding the Federal District): Campeche ($8^{1}/_2$ times), Nayarit ($2^{3}/_4$ times), Quintana Roo ($2^{1}/_4$ times) and Baja California Sur ($5^{1}/_4$ times). There does not appear to be any clear bias toward either richer or poorer states in the way general government investment spending is distributed.

Table 17. **Employment and taxes by state
and local governments in selected OECD countries**

1992

	Population Millions	Employment share [1]	Tax autonomy ratio [2]
Mexico	**85.6**	**40**	**1** [3]
United States	255.6	84	32
Japan	124.3	73	25
Germany	80.6	91	29
France	57.4	32	10
Italy	56.9	28	3
United Kingdom	58.0	53	4
Canada	28.4	70	43
Australia	17.5	82	23
Austria	7.9	62	22
Belgium	10.0	78	5
Denmark	5.2	79	31
Finland	5.0	77	21
Greece	10.3	11	1
The Netherlands	15.2	26	2
Norway	4.3	74	21
Portugal	9.9	17	6
Spain	39.1	47	12
Sweden	8.7	73	34
Switzerland	6.9	75	37
Turkey	58.4	14	8

1. Employment at sub-national levels of government as a percentage of employment at all levels of government excluding public enterprises, where identifiable.
2. Taxes at sub-national levels of government as a percentage of tax revenues of all levels of government (including social security).
3. 1991.
Source: OECD and INEGI, *Encuesta Nacional de la Dinamica Demográfica.*

The distribution may reflect different investment requirements, but it has also been suggested that these differences may be the result of some states having better and easier access to decision-making bodies.

Some decentralisation of education and health provision also took place during the Salinas administration, with the aim of improving the delivery of services by placing them in the hands of those with knowledge of local needs and priorities. However, these decentralisation efforts were not entirely successful. In education, administration of schools has been transferred to states along with specific funding, but teachers' pay, the major spending item in the education budget, is still negotiated at the federal level, which limits the capacity of the states to manage their budgets in an efficient manner. Before this decentralisation took place, some states had devoted a substantial part of their budget to education, while in others the federal government had been financing all education expenditures. In the national health system (*i.e.* that not managed by social security institutions), the transfer of operational responsibilities for health care services to state authorities has so far been less far reaching and only some 13 states have chosen to participate in the decentralised system.

The Zedillo administration is committed to undertaking reforms designed to bring about more fundamental redistribution of authority, resources and responsibility between the federal government, the states and municipalities. Reforms include changes to the Constitution that would give the states and municipalities the right to appeal to the Supreme Court over federal laws that will affect their region. Although the Constitution already officially gives municipalities sovereignty over their affairs, greater efforts are to be made to put this into practice.

Preparing these reforms is likely to take some time, as there are several questions to address in this context. The first issue is to ensure that the federal government's capacity to manage macroeconomic policy is not undermined as more resources and activities are devolved to the states and municipalities.[64] This may require negotiating an agreement on limits to the states' and municipalities' capacity to borrow, or establishing an effective incentive mechanism that discourages states from borrowing. The second issue is to ensure fiscal accountability, so that those responsible for the allocation of public resources are also clearly accountable to the electorate for the decisions they have taken. Where clear accountability is confused or even absent, the resulting incentive structure has little scope for promoting the efficient allocation of resources. The third issue is to find the most appropriate balance between encouraging flexibility and local decision-making in responding to local needs and priorities and ensuring that nation-wide objectives are still met. In education, for example, building of schools and employment conditions for teachers may well be best dealt with at the local level, but it may still be useful for the curriculum and minimum education standards to be set nation-wide as is the case in Mexico at present.[65] The fourth issue is to avoid a situation where the richer states stride ahead while the poorest states are left behind, unable to overcome their initial disadvantages. This suggests that even if poverty alleviation programmes are administered at local levels and involve the states and local community in identifying their needs and priorities, they should remain a federal responsibility. Finally, a transitional issue is the limited capacity of some states and municipalities to take on a significantly larger role and more functions in the immediate future, due to insufficient management skills, financial systems and administrative structures. Finding ways of providing the appropriate technical assistance to spread administrative infrastructure to those states and municipalities where it is currently missing is needed for successful decentralisation and effective federalism.

The monetary policy framework

The Mexican authorities have taken a number of steps in the early post-crisis period aimed at clarifying their monetary policy objectives and helping to ensure monetary discipline. These include quantitative restrictions on central bank credit and improvements in the transparency of monetary operations, discussed in Part II. The Bank of Mexico has also set out in broad terms its objectives for inflation reduction. In its January 1995 policy statement, the Bank announced objectives of reducing the inflation rate to less than 10 per cent by the end of 1996 (subsequently re-stated as an objective over a 2-3 year period), and to the 0-3 per cent range in the long term. These objectives are stated within the context of the Bank's autonomy and constitutional mandate to pursue price stability.

As the policy focus moves beyond management of the post-crisis adjustment, it will be important that the authorities build on these efforts and move towards a well-articulated policy framework in which the following key elements are more fully developed:

- the specification of a clear overriding policy objective consistent with low inflation in the medium term, endorsed by the executive and Congress;
- an operating system consistent with achieving that objective; and
- provision of information by the central bank concerning its ongoing assessment of economic and financial developments and their monetary policy implications.

A sound framework encompassing these areas is important for two reasons. First, it will ensure that problems of conflicting objectives in monetary policy are

71

avoided and that monetary policy over the medium term is directed unambiguously at achieving a satisfactory inflation performance. Second, it will help to promote confidence in financial markets by providing a sound basis for the formation of longer-run expectations; this is particularly important given Mexico's history of high inflation and the need to reassure investors that inflation will be resisted in the future. It is also important to promote a solid banking and payments system on which the operation of monetary policy crucially depends – an issue reviewed separately in Part IV.

As noted above, the monetary policy system now operating under a floating exchange rate recognises price stability as the ultimate objective, consistent with the Bank of Mexico's constitutional mandate. The Bank has stated that day-to-day policy operations will react to a range of indicators with the aim of ensuring that the conduct of policy is consistent with achievement of the objective over time. Such indicators include developments in the observed monetary base relative to its expected path (determined in conjunction with the price objective), inflation developments (particularly any deviation between expected inflation and the agreed objective), wage settlements, movements in the exchange rate relative to official projections and movements in the term structure of interest rates. The ceiling on the Central Bank's net domestic credit, which has been specified for 1995, is calculated by reference to a monetary base projection which is in turn derived from projections of real GDP growth and the inflation objective for that year.[66] The Bank of Mexico has full operational independence to implement monetary policy, although specification of the exchange rate regime is the prerogative of the government.

There are a number of respects in which it would be helpful to promote a better understanding of the policy framework among market participants and the general public, particularly given that the system of policy formulation under a floating exchange rate is relatively new and there is a need to build market confidence in the operation of the system. In particular, the framework by which developments in the indicator variables are translated into policy actions, and related to final objectives, could perhaps be more explicitly explained, along the lines practised in some other floating exchange-rate countries such as Canada. This might include a more detailed explanation of how movements in potentially conflicting indicators are assessed and what criteria are used in making judgements about their relative importance. Also relevant in this regard would be a fuller explanation of the role of the ceiling on net domestic credit expansion by the Central Bank in guiding policy decisions within the year. Such explanations could help to facilitate a better understanding of the rationale for policy actions as they are occurring, which may be important for market confidence when adjustments have to be made in the light of new information. In addition it will soon be time to specify the role of the net domestic credit variable in the policy framework for 1996. Although provision of information in all these areas is likely to be helpful in promoting confidence, the building up of a sound track record of inflation control will be necessary to policy credibility.

The role of a ceiling on the central bank's net domestic credit in the overall policy strategy has been a subject of some debate among market observers. The ceiling effectively puts a limit on the volume of net new central bank lending to financial intermediaries and to the federal government through purchases of securities. This framework was initially criticised by some observers on the basis that holdings of borrowed reserves under the international programme would artificially reduce net domestic credit, thereby significantly easing the degree of discipline implied by the ceiling. As was subsequently made clear to the markets, this criticism is not valid because borrowed reserves are to be excluded from the calculation. A further criticism is that by specifying this policy constraint in the form of a ceiling it is unclear to markets what is the central objective for this variable. A final point concerns the issue of whether or not net domestic credit is the correct variable to define central bank operations, since it is a difference between two balance-sheet items rather than a measure of the Bank's total balance-sheet size. In practice, however, the Bank of Mexico works on the assumption of stable foreign exchange reserves under a floating exchange rate, in which case the ceiling is conceptually equivalent to a constraint on growth of the monetary base.

The central priority in developing a consistent longer-term framework is to ensure that monetary policy is directed unambiguously at achieving satisfactorily low inflation. This raises issues concerning both the specification of the objective and its means of implementation. Concerning specification of the objective, key issues include how low an inflation rate would be regarded as satisfactorily low, how quickly to aim at reducing inflation to the desired range, what measure of inflation to focus on (for example, development of a measure of underlying inflation excluding volatile items), and how much temporary fluctuation in inflation rates would be regarded as acceptable in the longer run. At this stage the objectives set out by the Bank of Mexico (less than 10 per cent inflation within two to three years, and a 0 to 3 per cent range as a longer-term objective) seem broadly appropriate and, if achieved, would eventually bring Mexican inflation rates close to those of most other OECD countries. The exact definitions of the inflation rate and time periods to which these objectives refer are still unspecified. However, greater precision would probably not be realistic until the inflation rate moves closer to the desired range. As discussed below, there is a need, in view of current uncertainties, to avoid setting objectives for inflation reduction that are excessively ambitious or too tightly defined, since this could be counter-productive to policy credibility.

Implementation of the inflation objectives could in principle be achieved either through an external anchor (*i.e.* an exchange-rate commitment consistent with the objective) or through commitment to a system of internal monetary policy discipline. The discussion that follows argues that the latter is likely to be the more attractive option for Mexico in the foreseeable future, but that this could require further clarification of the monetary policy framework as outlined above.

An early return to any tight form of exchange rate peg is probably not feasible in Mexico, for several reasons. First, the Bank of Mexico's capacity to defend an exchange-rate commitment in the short run has been severely weakened by the crisis: foreign reserves are low, market confidence is still fragile, and the degree to which such an exchange-rate objective might conflict with internal monetary policy objectives in the short run is highly uncertain. In addition, there are considerable uncertainties about the nature and scope of the macroeconomic adjustments taking place in the post-crisis environment. These uncertainties relate to the short-run effects of the crisis on prices and output as well as on the health of the banking sector, all of which could contribute to unforeseen exchange-rate pressures. A more general point is that, having observed Mexico's failure to achieve a smooth "re-entry" after using the exchange rate as a disinflationary device, markets are likely to be doubly sceptical of a further attempt to do the same thing. A minimum precondition for any possible return to a pegged exchange-rate system would be a reasonable degree of macroeconomic stability, which would probably have to include a fairly high degree of inflation convergence with the United States.

There are arguments on both sides of the issue of eventually returning to some form of exchange-rate commitment. A fixed exchange rate (presumably to the US dollar) would support longer-term monetary discipline and provide a safeguard against discretionary inflationary policies, as long as the commitment to maintaining the exchange rate is sufficiently strong. Re-building a track record of keeping to an exchange-rate commitment could help to restore financial market confidence. These potential advantages have to be balanced against the loss of monetary autonomy that would be involved, and the risks of further macroeconomic divergences generating renewed pressures on an exchange-rate commitment. Thus the choice of exchange-rate system must depend in part on whether satisfactory internal mechanisms to enforce monetary discipline can be found which would make an exchange rate commitment unnecessary for the maintenance of monetary credibility. Another important consideration is the behaviour of domestic wages and prices. If the setting of prices and wages is not sufficiently disciplined or responsive to market forces, a fixed exchange rate could be subject to the risk of cumulative losses of international competitiveness, and would therefore be more difficult or costly to sustain.

A number of commentators have advocated the introduction of a fixed exchange rate backed by a currency board in Mexico, possibly even as an immediate measure.[67] The basis of this advocacy is a view that a fixed exchange rate offers the best chance of restoring financial confidence, that the advantage of a fixed exchange rate for financial stability would outweigh any short-term need for policy flexibility, and that the operational features of a currency board would make such a system highly resistant to speculative attacks or loss of monetary discipline. The main elements of currency-board systems are the requirement of at least 100 per cent backing of the monetary base with liquid foreign exchange reserves, and that monetary operations of the currency board (the sole domestic monetary authority) would be limited to meeting demands for conversion between domestic and foreign currency at the official exchange rate; in other words, it would eliminate all discretion at the operational level of monetary policy. Proponents argue that such a system would provide a credible guarantee of convertibility at the official exchange rate.

Critics of currency boards point to two main sources of problems. First, the elimination of operational policy flexibility might have important costs if there are large macroeconomic divergences from the anchor country, as is likely to be the case with Mexico in the near-term future. Second, foreign-reserve backing of substantially more than 100 per cent of the monetary base might be needed to guarantee convertibility in practice. The reason for this is that any fear of depreciation would be likely to lead to a degree of substitution into foreign currency from both the domestic monetary base and from other liquid domestic-currency assets. Without sufficient foreign reserves to back a substantial propor-tion of the deposit base of the banking system and the stock of short-term government debt, a currency board could not guarantee convertibility in the event of a major run without inducing illiquidity of the banks and government. Recent experience with Argentina's currency-board system, where banks have faced serious liquidity shortages, illustrate the reality of this problem. At a practical level, Mexico might find it difficult to mobilise sufficient foreign exchange reserves to allow immediate establishment of a currency board capable of meet-ing these types of contingencies.

It is possible to envisage a range of other policy approaches centred around the exchange rate but involving lesser degrees of commitment to exchange rate stability. At the "tight" end of such a range of options would be a hard-edged exchange-rate band consistent with low inflation, combined with a strong com-mitment not to modify the band or to deviate from it. Intermediate or looser options would include crawling bands set in conjunction with inflation targets (as in Israel), systems of continuously adjustable bands (such as the one currently operating in Chile), informal target zones with unspecified edges, or target bands that are sufficiently wide as to avoid representing a strong constraint on policy.[68] In the light of Mexico's recent experience it is hard to view policy approaches centred around the exchange rate as likely to be attractive as a basis for policy in the near future. A tight exchange-rate band would suffer from many of the same difficulties discussed above in association with a fixed exchange rate: in particu-lar, the difficulty of credibly defending such a band in the face of current uncertainties. A looser band would run the risk of failing to provide a convincing nominal anchor, unless clearly placed within a credible framework of inflation targeting.

Given the likely difficulties of an early move to a policy based on exchange rate commitments, and the need for a clear framework to help rebuild monetary policy credibility, the most promising option for Mexico might be to move towards a system of formal inflation targets along the lines of other OECD countries such as Canada, New Zealand or the United Kingdom, under which policy would respond to a range of indicators of inflationary pressures. Such an approach could build on efforts already made by the Bank of Mexico to define medium-term inflation objectives. Experience with inflation-control targets in a number of other OECD countries can give some guidance as to how such a system would work. Although institutional details vary considerably from country to country, such systems have a number of key features in common: these include the specification of a numerical inflation objective by the government, delegation of responsibility for achieving the objective to a central bank with operational independence, and accountability by the central bank for its implementation of the policy. This overall framework leaves room for distinctive national approaches to such issues as the specification of ranges as opposed to point targets, the exact nature of central bank reporting systems, and the specification of conditions under which targets are subject to modification. A crucial requirement is to develop a system of intermediate indicators and forecasts of inflation to permit timely policy reactions to unfolding events.

A key problem that Mexico would face in moving towards such an inflation-targeting system would be to define an objective that is sufficiently tight to constrain future policies without being unrealistically ambitious. Credibility will not be enhanced by setting goals that are perceived as being too tight to be attainable. This problem has been faced in some degree by all countries adopting inflation-targeting, but it is one that is likely to require particularly difficult judgements where a large reduction in inflation is being sought and the evolution of future inflationary pressures is highly uncertain, as in Mexico. This suggests that any inflation-targeting commitment would need to be stated in relatively broad terms, but terms which nonetheless constrain inflation to a satisfactory downward path over a definable period – perhaps something along the lines already put forward by the Bank of Mexico, and possibly including a statement of conditions under which the targets would be modifiable in the future.

An advantage of inflation-targeting systems is that they allow flexibility to respond to shocks. In Mexico's case, the economy is likely to be exposed to shocks with divergent effects *vis-à-vis* the United States (for example, an oil-price shock) which could be partly absorbed by exchange-rate movements. However, such flexibility comes at the cost of foregoing the more-or-less automatic discipline imposed by an exchange-rate commitment. To underpin credibility it is therefore important that any inflation-targeting system be supported by an institutional structure conducive to disciplined adherence to the targets. A central requirement is that the target adopted be formally endorsed by the government. In addition a number of other institutional steps could be helpful in Mexico if a stricter inflation-targeting system were to be adopted. These are:

- re-orientation of the Bank's regular policy reports so that explanations of policy actions would be more explicitly related to the inflation targets; and
- improvements in the Bank's economic monitoring capacity and information base by which the development of inflationary pressures can be assessed.

Development of a system of intermediate indicators and more tightly focused policy reports would be important from the point of view of both public accountability and quality of decision-making. Such a system would help to make clear how the objective with respect to inflation control is being operationalised, and would facilitate monitoring by financial markets of adherence to the targets. To support such a system there is a need in Mexico for more timely and comprehensive information on economic developments. Publication lags are long in a number of areas including monetary and credit statistics, national accounts, employment and other indicators of real activity, and there is a lack of comprehensive information in key areas including non-bank financial intermediation, business financing and timely indicators of short-term developments.

IV. Progress in structural reform

For over 10 years Mexico has engaged in a process of wide-ranging structural reform, with the aim of making its economy more open, more flexible and more responsive to market forces. The role of the State has been reduced, with considerable disengagement from areas of policy intervention in which markets are deemed to be better suited to deliver economic growth. At the same time, as in the rest of the OECD area, the authorities have increasingly recognised the need to improve their ability to provide markets with an appropriate regulatory framework in which to operate. Progress made in structural reforms in the late 1980s and early 1990s was reviewed in the 1992 *Economic Survey of Mexico*. This chapter is devoted to more recent measures implemented or announced in a number of areas, notably privatisation and competition policy, financial liberalisation, agricultural reform and possible improvements to the functioning of labour markets.

Privatisation, deregulation and competition policy

The extent of the rolling back of the State from direct production of goods and services has been impressive. In terms of both receipts from divestitures and the range of industries in which ownership was transferred to private hands, Mexico ranks high among OECD countries (Table 18). After a first phase (1982-88), when mostly small and medium-sized enterprises were sold or liquidated, the privatisation drive gathered momentum during the Salinas administration and major public companies were sold.[69] Over the last 2 years, the State has divested its interests in the media and insurance businesses and has sold Miconsa, the country's second-largest cornflower producer (Table 19). The number of State-owned enterprises declined from 1 155 to less than 200. The sell-off of public enterprises fetched a cumulated US$23.7 billion in the 1988-94 period (as

Table 18. **Privatisations in selected countries**

	Airlines	Railways	Electricity	Steel	Telecoms
Mexico	PR	TBP	TBP	PR	PR
United States	P	P	M	P	P
Germany	S[1]	S	M	P	S
France	S	S	S	S	S
Italy	S[1]	S	TBP	PR	TBP[1]
United Kingdom	PR	TBP	PR	PR	PR
Australia	TBP[1]	S	S	P	S
New Zealand	PR	PR	S	PR	PR
Chile	PR	PR	PR	PR	PR
Korea	S	S	S[1]	S	S[1]

M = mixed private and public ownership.
P = private ownership.
PR = privatised.
S = public ownership.
TBP = to be privatised by end 1996.
1. Partly privatised (minority stakes).
Source: OECD.

a point of reference, the 1992 GDP was US$196 billion). Receipts were placed in a special contingency fund, and were generally used for public debt redemption. On the other hand, privatisations have been less successful in extending share ownership among the population at large and at decreasing concentration in Mexican economic power. While the total number of stock holders has grown from very low levels, in the absence of well-developed private pension and mutual funds – as existed in the United Kingdom or Chile – wide share-ownership and ''people's capitalism'' have proved to be difficult to attain.

Following the adoption of the emergency stabilisation plan in early 1995, the government announced a new privatisation round. The list includes manufacturing plants operating in competitive markets (petrochemicals) as well as utilities and public services (satellite communications, railways, electricity, and seaports).[70] As regards PEMEX, the state-owned enterprise, over the last few years it has given priority to its core business, retrenching from secondary petrochemical activities, and the private share has correspondingly risen, to over 3/4 of total investment in petrochemicals in 1993. The government intends to pursue more aggressively the privatisation of non-core PEMEX activities, but has firmly and repeatedly ruled out the possibility of allowing private-sector participation in oil

Table 19. Main privatisations in Mexico since 1991

US$ million

Year	Company	Sector	Equity share (per cent)	Amount	Foreign exchange	Purchaser
1991	Banca Cremi	Banking	66.7	241	–	Multivalores
1991	Banco Nacional de México (Banamex)	Banking	70.7	3 131	–	Acciones y Valores
1991	Empresas Gamesa	Beverage	70.0	320	320	Pepsi Cola
1991	Bancomer	Banking	51.0[1]	2 516	638	Valores Monterrey
1991	Teléfonos de México (TELMEX)	Telecommunications	15.7[2]	2 363	2 363	Grupo Carso, France Telecom, Southwestern Bell
1991	Teléfonos de México	Telecommunications	5.0	467	467	Southwestern Bell
1992	Multibanco Comermex	Banking	66.5	873	–	Agustín Legorreta Group
1992	Banco Internacional	Banking	72.0	480	–	Grupo Financiero Privado Mexicano
1992	Banco del Atlántico	Banking	68.6	474	–	Grupo Bursatil Americano
1992	Banco Mexicano Somex	Banking	81.6	605	–	Grupo Inverméxico
1992	Banca Serfín	Banking	51.0	912	–	Grupo Financiero OBSA
1992	Banco Mercantil del Norte	Banking	66.0	573	–	Grupo Maseca
1993	Aseguradora Mexicana	Insurance	51.0	582	–	Grupo Mexival Banpaís
1993	Channels 7 and 13	Television	100.0	645	–	Grupo Electra
1994	Teléfonos de México	Telecommunications	n.a.	550[3]	–	–

1. General Deposit Receipts.
2. American Deposit Receipts for 1 600 "L" shares (non-voting).
3. Convertible offering.

Source: OECD and Sader, F. (1993), "Privatisation and Foreign Investment in the Developing World, 1988-92", The World Bank, *WPS 1202.*

81

extraction. Article 27 of the Constitution was amended in 1995 to allow for private-sector participation in the transport, storage and distribution of natural gas. Sales of petrochemical gas plants are currently being prepared, with auctioning rules expected to be announced in 1996. Taking account of normal delays in preparing complex privatisation operations and the prevailing market sentiment, the original revenue targets were revised in March. Proceeds are now expected to be in the range of US$12-14 billion within the next three years.

The core area of economic activities in which the public sector intends to keep a role has been defined clearly through successive revision of the Constitution.[71] There does not appear to be ambiguity about the scope for State retrenchment in Mexico, unlike for instance in the case of Italy.[72] On the other hand, although deemed desirable, liberalisation in the provision of public services will require a long gestation period, in order for Mexican regulatory bodies to acquire the necessary skills, drawing on international experience. Up to now, Mexican authorities have indeed been rather timid in this domain: international experience shows that the opening up of public utilities to market forces (structure regulation) is easier before privatisation takes place rather than after, and that extensive conduct regulation to prevent abuses represents a second-best solution (Bishop *et al.*, 1995). However, new privatisations are to be supervised by a newly-created interministerial commission, with a mandate to introduce a competitive environment prior to privatisation.

Following the ownership change, the regulatory framework applied in telecoms has been insufficient (compared with other countries, including the United Kingdom and Chile), with no requirement other than in terms of new investment and increases in the number of lines in service (see Annex I, Table A2). Regulatory competences remained within the Ministry, no price-cap was introduced to reduce telephone tariffs as these had considerably lagged behind in real terms in the previous period, and sizeable profits in long-distance services (both domestic and international) have allowed continued subsidisation of urban customers.[73] The exclusive concession enjoyed by Telmex in long-distance services is due to expire in August 1996, with no limit on the number of carriers which can enter into the market thereafter although concessionaries will have to have a majority Mexican stake.[74] According to the law approved in mid-1995, new entrants will be allowed to set their own rates – whereas Telmex will have its tariffs capped for a period of 6 years – and to freely establish their own fibre-optic or cable networks, negotiating interconnection fees with Telmex for using the latter's fixed network. The bill seems conducive to a competitive market environment and it envisages the creation of an independent regulatory body, by no later than 10 August 1996, with decision-taking power and a mandate to develop an efficient telecommunications sector in Mexico. A price-cap to reduce telephone tariffs charged by the incumbent company is also to be introduced by early 1997.

While the Constitution preserves public monopoly in the electricity sector, a 1992 law has eased the terms for private-sector investment, by enabling private concerns to build and own plants. Self-consumption and co-generation have therefore become possible, but private producers remain obliged to sell the excess power they generate to the Federal Electricity Commission (CFE).[75]

Build-Operate-Transfer (BOT) schemes have been introduced in the water treatment sector. Under these, private operators pay for the treatment plants, and in return are given management and ownership with a guaranteed amount of business for a set number of years. Concerns about the ability of municipalities to pay the operator the agreed price for treating water have hindered the raising of debt collaterised by future revenues. In two cities (Aguascalientes and Cancun), private companies have been given management and ownership of the full water system for a fixed period.

In the road-infrastructure area, the government handed over the construction of all four-lane toll roads to the private sector in the early 1990s, with financing usually assured by the state (15 per cent), banks or capital markets (50 per cent) and private investors or construction companies for the rest. So far, the temporary concessions programme has been plagued by the poor performance of many of the roads, with traffic use well below projections (partly due to very high toll rates) and construction costs far above. The attempt by the past administration to achieve success within its term created a sense of urgency which was reflected in hastily-prepared traffic and cost projections and road designs.[76]

The airport infrastructure sector has also been opened up. Private capital increased from 5 per cent of 1989 investment to 72 per cent in 1993 – when it accounted for 16.5 per cent of total assets.[77] The sale of concessions to manage the country's 61 airports is expected.

Mexican ports have been decentralised since 1992. Progressive privatisation has reduced the role of the federal agency traditionally responsible for all aspects of port management and tariff setting (Puertos Mexicanos). Management was transferred to newly-created Integrated Port Authorities (APIs). New rules are expected in the course of the year, allowing APIs to negotiate wharfage rates directly with steamship lines, under general guidelines on maximum rates.[78] International tenders were invited in February 1995 for handling services in the country's four main ports (Manzanillo, Lazaro Cardenas, Veracruz and Altamira).

Finally, a law issued in 1995 aims at increasing operating efficiency and investment in railways through the awarding of long-term concessions on groups of lines to private Mexican investors, eventually associated with foreign ones. U.S. railways might actively participate in such tenders, in order to take advantage of the opportunities provided by increased bilateral trade flows. Concession packages and mechanisms to allow competition between different routes and types of services are being studied. In April 1995, the Mexican Congress approved reforms to allow private investments in the construction and operation of natural gas pipelines and in local distribution. The government is currently drafting the corresponding regulations. Private investments in the natural gas business will enhance international trade in this commodity and promote the substitution of fuel oil for a more environmentally friendly input.

Mexico issued a new federal competition law in 1993, recognising that privatisation and trade liberalisation, while necessary, are insufficient to ensure market competition. This law replaced direct controls (State ownership, price controls, exclusive concessions granted without due attention to competition criteria) with an explicit and more transparent regulatory approach. The newly-established Federal Competition Commission evaluates mergers, *ex officio* investigates possible anti-competitive practices, and assesses private suits filed in connection with alleged anti-competitive practices; it is also empowered to issue opinions on the effects that federal programmes and plans may have on competition.[79] The Commission enjoys budgetary autonomy and its five commissioners are named by the President of the Republic, who also appoints one of them as the Commission's president. In its first year of operation, the Commission has investigated and found evidence of anti-competitive behaviour in some highly-visible sectors, such as petrol station franchises, credit card operations, government securities auctions by banks, and dry-cleaning services, fining the firms involved.

Financial reforms

Mexico's financial system has gone through a process of deep reorganisation in recent years, a result of deregulation, bank privatisation and opening to foreign competition,[80] with further major structural changes likely to result from adjustment to the post-crisis environment. Key stages in the recent reform process have been:

- a series of measures to allow banks to issue short-term securities at market interest rates and to participate fully in government securities markets (October-November 1988);
- deregulation of banks' deposit and lending interest rates (1989);
- easing of cross-ownership restrictions to allow the formation of financial groups that might include banks, insurance companies, securities brokers and other specialist institutions (1989);
- the elimination of mandatory credit allocation and reserve requirements (1989), as well as liquidity ratios (1991);
- a constitutional amendment allowing private ownership of banks, paving the way for full privatisation of the commercial banking sector between 1991 and 1993;
- adoption of bank capital standards based on the Basle accord (1991-1993); and
- a significant, phased opening of the financial sector, which was accelerated as of January 1994, in accordance with NAFTA provisions.

As in many other OECD countries, financial deregulation was driven both by an active desire to improve efficiency as part of a broader programme of market-based reforms, and by the need to react to the increasing ineffectiveness of the previous regulatory system arising from rapid growth of the less regulated parts of the financial sector. In Mexico's case, tight controls on bank interest rates and heavy reliance on bank reserve requirements to finance the fiscal deficit had led to the development of a large informal financial market, which created strong pressures for reforms to allow the banks to compete. An important consequence of the overall reform process has been the shift to reliance on open market operations rather than direct controls in the conduct of monetary policy.

NAFTA should provide a spur to structural change by opening Mexico's financial markets to foreign competition. The main provisions of the agreement, as it applies to the financial services sector, are that banks from NAFTA countries will be allowed to establish operations in Mexico on a national treatment basis (*i.e.* under the same regulations as domestic institutions), subject to foreign market-share limits that will be gradually phased out by December 1999. The rule of origin for NAFTA banks is the place of incorporation, regardless of the investor's nationality. This means that foreign financial institutions with a subsidiary in Canada or the United States will be able to establish in Mexico through their subsidiaries. Other parts of the financial sector including insurance and brokerage companies will also be open to increased participation by institutions from NAFTA countries.

By February 1995, there had been 102 applications under NAFTA provisions for the establishment of financial businesses by foreign subsidiaries, of which 39 were successful. As discussed in Part II, under the policy measures approved by the Congress in early 1995, the foreign market share limit under NAFTA provisions will only be lifted for those foreign banks that take over domestic ones: this relaxation is intended to promote foreign investment to help recapitalise the domestic banking sector, whose capital base has been damaged by the crisis.

Financial deregulation has been associated with a rapid growth of the Mexican financial sector. Two indicators of this growth – stock market capitalisation and banking-sector assets relative to GDP – are shown in Figure 15. These suggest that the overall scale of private-sector debt and equity markets have more than doubled in relation to GDP since the late 1980s, although to some extent these increases are boosted by the impact of privatisation as well as re-absorption by banks of much of the informal financial sector.[81] Despite the rapid expansion, Mexico's financial sector remains relatively under-developed compared with other OECD countries on these measures, as well as in terms of other indicators such as the extent of bank branch networks (Table 20). The Mexican banking system also appears to have a relatively high cost structure. Net interest margins in 1993 and 1994 were over 5 percentage points, compared with an average of 2.6 percentage points in other OECD countries for which comparable figures are available;[82] staff costs were also somewhat higher. This background suggests there could be considerable scope for bank profitability to be improved through greater cost-efficiency, and that there may be attractive entry and investment opportunities in Mexico for foreign banks.

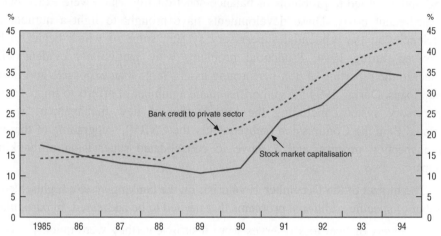

Figure 15. **SIZE OF THE FINANCIAL SECTOR**

Per cent of GDP[1]

1. End-of-period values as per cent of annual GDP. For 1994, November values and projected GDP.
Source: Banco de México and Fédération Internationale des Bourses de Valeurs.

Table 20. **Financial sector structural indicators, 1993**

Percentages unless otherwise indicated

	Mexico	United States	Canada	Spain	Turkey	South Korea
Money stock (M3)/GDP	41	67	59	97	16	42
Banking sector						
Total assets/GDP	53	91	103	161	39	118
Branches (per 100 000 inhabitants)	5	39	61	88	11	12
Net interest margin	6.3	3.9	2.9	3.4	11.5	2.8
Staff costs/total assets	2.1	1.6	1.5	1.6	3.4	1.3
Operating costs/total assets[1]	4.0	3.9	2.7	2.7	4.7	1.8
Stock market						
Capitalisation (per cent of GDP)	35	67	59	21	12	36
Number of stocks listed[2]	190	1 946	1 193	378	160	693
Insurance premia/GDP[3]	1.5	10.1	5.0	4.1	1.1	11.6

1. Operating costs include personnel and administrative costs and depreciation.
2. For the United States, Canada and Spain, data refer to the New York, Toronto and Madrid Stock Exchanges respectively.
3. 1992, except Korea (1993).
Source: OECD (1994), *Bank Profitability, Insurance Statistics Yearbook, Main Economic Indicators*; IMF (1994), *International Financial Statistics*; Comisión Nacional Bancaria; and Fédération Internationale des Bourses de Valeurs, *Statistics 1993*.

87

As was discussed in Part II, excessive financial-sector expansion between 1988 and 1994 led to problems of balance-sheet quality which were exacerbated by the recent crisis. These developments have brought to light a number of deficiencies in the prudential supervisory system, some of which began to be addressed during 1994. Prudential problems were particularly evident with respect to the reporting of non-performing assets, large loan exposures and intra-group loans. During 1994 the authorities made a number of efforts to improve the supervisory system, including the introduction of new management at the National Banking Commission (subsequently the CNBV),[83] upgrading of the on-site inspection process, and a move to consolidated supervision of banking groups.[84]

The impact of the December 1994 crisis on the banking system highlighted a number of specific additional problems that needed to be addressed. In particular:

- levels of loan-loss reserves were insufficient (they were quickly raised following the crisis);
- past-due loans were reported under principles which differed from international accounting standards. This resulted in under-estimation of the deterioration of loan portfolios; and
- safeguards issued by the central bank against excessive indirect exchange-rate exposures, through foreign-currency loans to domestic borrowers without a hedge, were violated by some commercial banks that will be sanctioned accordingly.

Although efforts to upgrade prudential standards will take some time to be fully implemented, measures adopted in early 1995 went some way towards addressing the first two of these problems by increasing minimum loan-loss reserves and requiring reporting to the supervisory authorities based on international accounting standards.[85] A move to require public disclosure on this basis is currently under discussion and planned for implementation next year. Concerning the third issue, there appears to be a need for stronger enforcement of prudential rules with respect to banks' foreign-currency loan exposures.

The banking sector is likely to remain under strain for a considerable period of time while its capital base is being re-built. There is a limit to how much an improved supervisory system can contribute to this recovery process, which will depend importantly on recovery in the economy more widely. Nonetheless, improved supervisory standards can make an important contribution to improving the soundness of the financial sector beyond the current cycle, as well as helping to ensure that fiscal costs of bank support operations are kept to a minimum. It is important therefore that current efforts to upgrade the expertise of the supervisory agencies, to improve disclosure standards, and to limit excessive concentrations of risk, should be continued.

Mexico's insurance sector is relatively small by international standards, with total insurance premia of only 1.5 per cent of GDP compared with around 4 per cent in Spain and 10 per cent in the United States. At present, only 2 per cent of the population owns a life insurance policy and only around one quarter of the automobile stock carries liability insurance. High costs appear to have kept the number of insured buildings relatively low despite the fact that the country is highly exposed to seismic risks. As in other parts of the financial sector, the opening to foreign investors as a result of NAFTA could lead to a significant increase in the supply of services.

The main priorities for further reform in the financial sector are likely to be to continue the process of market opening, and to improve the framework of bank prudential supervision. Financial market opening is beginning to improve the operating efficiency of the financial sector and should therefore contribute to higher private saving rates. Increased foreign equity participation is helping to alleviate current problems of capital shortage in the banking sector. Implementation of a thorough reform of prudential policies under the CNBV will take some time to complete, but continued efforts in this area will be important in ensuring that the banking sector emerges from the current crisis on a sound footing.

Agricultural reforms

Major reforms have been introduced in the agricultural sector over the last decade or so: removal of most price subsidies, liberalisation of trade, especially through GATT and NAFTA, rationalisation and privatisation of several marketing and processing institutions, and definition of a new legal framework for land tenure and property rights. But the size of the underlying problems to be addressed after a long history of inward orientation and inefficient public intervention has meant that progress in the performance of the agricultural sector has yet to be discernible. While in the 1980s the rural population has grown more slowly than agricultural GDP (including livestock and forestry), poverty in rural areas remains widespread. Nearly a quarter of the labour force is engaged in agricultural activities, but the sector accounts for only 7 per cent of GDP. The agricultural trade balance has shown erratic performance with a trend towards mounting deficit, reaching a record high of nearly US$1 billion in 1994 (US$3 billion if processed food and beverages are included). The agricultural sector is dualistic, with a vast number of farmers on small plots of rain-fed land, mainly in the South, who often produce for own consumption and earn incomes close to or below subsistence level, co-existing with a modern sector of large plots of irrigated land, mainly in the North-West, where farmers have access to credit, better technology and sell their products on domestic and international markets.[86]

One of the fundamental reforms of the last few years has been to establish conditions, through the change in 1992 to Article 27 of the Constitution, which allow increased private land ownership and a greater degree of certainty in property. The reform makes it possible for *ejido* farmers (those jointly owning common lands) under certain conditions to own, sell, rent or mortgage *ejido* land.[87] It eliminates the legal prohibition against the formation of productive associations with other producers or business, while limiting foreign investors to minority participation in *ejido* capital. To avoid excessive concentration of land ownership and the emergence of large latifundia, limits on maximum property size have been established together with regulations.[88] Land titling relies on a very time-consuming surveying and title-production process. Given the high fragmentation of land tenure and difficult access to many of the areas concerned, implementation of the reform has been slower than expected: the Programme for certification of *ejido* rights (PROCEDE), which was supposed to be well advanced by 1994, has fallen behind schedule. Budgetary constraints in 1995 make it impossible to accelerate the process this year. The land tenure reform, however, risks benefiting primarily commercial *ejidarios*, the largest ones in particular, because possession of a title should ensure them access to credit and external investment. For the vast majority of subsistence farmers, the reform by itself may have little impact, and other government actions (such as basic public works, technical assistance, training), as well as improved access to social services, will continue.

A second element of the reforms has been the process of trade liberalisation – the latest step being NAFTA – including the reduction in the proportion of agricultural import subject to licensing and a swift fall of the average tariff for agricultural produce. The average producer subsidy equivalents over 14 major commodities correspondingly fell from 47.6 per cent in the mid-1980s to 19.9 per cent in 1990 (USDA, 1994).[89] In the NAFTA Agreement, the countries' structural differences were explicitly recognised only in the market access area. Tariffs and tariff-free import quotas have been established for transition periods. Domestic support programmes, export subsidies, sanitary and phyto-sanitary regulations are also covered.[90]

A third pillar has been the elimination of guaranteed price for all basic foodstuffs, except maize and beans. Subsidies on most inputs (including fertilisers, water and electricity) and on credit were scaled down at the same time, and State intervention and market control on sugar, cocoa, maize, tobacco and sisal were eliminated or reduced. PROCAMPO was launched in 1994 to fully replace over a 15-year period the system of price support for basic grains (including maize and beans), which was to be phased out. It provides direct cash payments on an area-basis to producers, regardless of the kind of crops or the amount they produce. PROCAMPO's goal is to compensate for the combined effect of the reduction in price support and the elimination of trade barriers through NAFTA that is expected to entail costly adjustment on the rural population[91] – as well as to compensate for the subsidies given to producers in other countries. The 1994 PROCAMPO budget was US$3.5 billion, twice the programmed cost of the price support scheme; but a major difference is that the burden is now shared among all taxpayers, whereas previously consumers were bearing the cost. A further advantage of PROCAMPO is that it distributes some income to small producers who benefited little from the guaranteed price scheme. In 1994, 3.3 million agricultural producers are estimated to have benefited from the payments, of which 2.2 million previously lacked any type of support.[92] However useful PROCAMPO may be during the transition period, it is nevertheless a very costly programme that may be insufficiently targeted to smaller farmers and could delay some of the public investments that are much needed to boost productivity in the longer term. The depreciation of the peso has corrected the foreign-exchange distortion that made imports artificially cheap and harmed domestic producers. Current conditions appear to be conducive to a removal of remaining price controls on grains and a correction of the remaining price distortions. The reduction or elimination of the price gap between world and

domestic crop prices would have the additional advantage of reducing government subsidies and allowing savings to be made by removing the bureaucracy in
charge of the current system. These savings could then be used in other areas.

Landless workers (some 3 million people) will not benefit directly from
PROCAMPO, and the demand for their labour is expected to be reduced by
liberalisation policies. However, they will benefit from lower food prices. As
with subsistence farmers, many landless labourers are likely to leave the sector,
thereby creating migration pressures towards urban areas. Government programmes are needed to provide alternative sources of income to alleviate these
pressures. A wide range of actions could be envisaged to assist subsistence
farmers and landless labourers:

- develop more effective mechanisms to deliver financial services;[93]
- support the Solidarity programmes (FONAES and Production funds)
  that have a high grant element and improve their targeting;
- implement public investment programmes for irrigation in rain-fed areas
  and for rural road maintenance, which would also serve to provide
  employment, at least temporarily, thus alleviating hardship; and
- design training programmes.

In the longer run, the creation of employment opportunities in small- and
medium-size cities will be needed to stem further rural-urban migration. This is
part of the government's strategy as announced in the National Development
Plan.

Improving the functioning of the labour market

In Mexico, unlike most other OECD countries, labour market problems do
not manifest themselves so much in high open unemployment, but rather in low
productivity of a significant share of the labour force and uneven access to job
opportunities. The main characteristics can be summarised as follows:

- The labour market is, at least formally, highly regulated. Social contributions total 30 per cent of wages. The duration of a work relationship is
  considered to be indefinite and severance payments (equal to three
  months of salary, plus 12 days of salary for each year of service)

constitute an additional cost and limit job mobility. Non-compliance, however, is a widespread phenomenon, even in the formal sector.

- The labour code provides for a minimum wage, but its incidence is small (Bell, 1994):[94] its real level has fallen steadily since 1982, to about one-ninth of the average manufacturing wage for unskilled labour; and by 1994 the proportion of employees earning the minimum wage had fallen below 15 per cent.

- There is no general unemployment insurance. On the other hand, the compulsory saving system for retirement, created in 1992 and funded through employers' contributions, allows participants, under certain conditions, to draw on their savings during unemployment spells. Severance pay in the formal sector can also provide subsistence means to displaced workers during job-search.

- A large share of the workforce is poorly qualified; moreover, adult illiteracy remains a major problem, hampering efforts to improve productivity.[95] As a consequence, it is an absolute priority to upgrade skills through a more effective system of vocational and on-the-job training, as well as schemes to retrain displaced workers.[96]

- The segmentation of the economy into a formal and an informal sector (the latter accounting for an estimated 35 per cent of total non-farm employment) constitutes a major problem on both efficiency and equity grounds.[97] The two sectors are markedly different in terms of workforce qualifications and working conditions, the formal sector being relatively privileged in terms of job security, wages, health insurance and other social security benefits. There are also two standards with respect to the enforcement of legislation on health and safety conditions and child labour.

Deregulating the labour market

A reform of employment and social security provisions might be desirable, and is indeed included in the 1995 National Development Plan. Real wage flexibility in the 1980s possibly explains why improving the functioning of the labour market was not seen as an urgent requirement in the early 1990s. The adoption of reforms leading to more flexible working relations, potentially easing the absorption of hitherto marginalised segments of the population, was probably hampered in the past by the strong influence of trade unions. Moving towards more open forms of labour representation would facilitate reforms: indeed, as the World Bank recently suggested, there is a vast array of policy measures that governments can take to enhance the welfare of workers, in the formal and informal sectors alike.[98] Provisions concerning the assignment of tasks, promotions, the duration of contracts and the right for the employer to dismiss workers also seem unduly restrictive (where the legislation is enforced). However, the deregulation of employment security provisions would need to be accompanied by improvements in the coverage of the safety net.

An area where deregulation is probably easier to accomplish and is warranted to produce considerable social welfare gains is that of small- and micro-enterprises. The application of all provisions included in the labour legislation to all enterprises, regardless of their size, risks making such firms economically unviable, thereby pushing them to informality. There is indeed a strong argument for modifying both compensation payments and the modalities for social security coverage in accordance with capacity, as this would stimulate the creation of new enterprises and new jobs, and allow a shift of a number of existing enterprises from the informal to the formal sector (Ozorio de Almeida *et al.*, 1994). While initiatives in this direction have been taken in recent years – such as the provision of special forms of legal association, the introduction of a simplified tax regime to bring micro-enterprises into the tax base and the easing of bureaucratic procedures through the creation of a single operational centre (*Ventanilla Unica de Gestión*) – the vast majority of microfirms has still to experience any tangible results.

Upgrading skills and competences

While technical education and training offered by the public sector's *Sistema Nacional de Educación Tecnológica* reaches no less than one million students, the system is plagued by problems – such as its supply-driven nature, uneven quality of programmes and insufficient private-sector involvement – that severely limit its effectiveness. An integrated effort is needed along the following lines, some of which have already been incorporated in the government's programmes and announcements:

– introduce standardised competency and skill tests;

- certify public and private training organisations as eligible to compete for both direct training contracts from enterprises and public training contracts;
- make courses more flexible, with modular units that allow students to participate only in activities that they value most, and improve access to such courses in rural and peri-urban areas;
- improve the co-ordination between pre- and in-service training (for youths before entering the labour market and for employed workers, respectively) by introducing an apprenticeship system;[99]
- develop co-operation between the government and the business sector in the design, running and evaluation of such programmes, so as to make them more demand-driven and improve their impact upon earnings;
- make a greater effort in targeting programmes, such as PROBECAT, so that they reach users who stand to benefit the most,[100] and increase resources devoted to providing teaching in basic literacy skills as a first step toward technical training; and
- continue with the effort of offering scholarships, in addition to the 700 000 that have been granted by CIMO and PROBECAT.

Reforming the social security system

Social security benefits – health and maternity insurance, disability and retirement pensions, and babies' day-care – are provided in Mexico by a variety of institutions, of which the most important are the Mexican Social Security Institute (IMSS), the Social Security Institute for State Employees (ISSSTE), and those for Pemex employees and the Armed Forces. While the system, the IMSS in particular, has reached many of its targets since its creation in the 1940s, widening the share of the population covered and assuring social services to the working class, it suffers from a plethora of problems:

- more than half of Mexico's population, namely peasants, domestic workers and the self-employed, are not covered;
- contributions constitute a heavy burden, which may possibly deter job creation in the formal economy, as well as induce collusion between employers and employees in order to evade payments; and
- the IMSS bureaucracy, considerable in size of payroll and budget, suffers from inefficiencies and provides services of sub-optimal quality.

A further element is the rapid demographic transition taking place in Mexico the population, although much younger than in most other OECD countries, is or an ageing trend and the dependency ratio is expected to grow rapidly as the number of pensioners grows at more than twice the rate of young people entering the workforce.

The new administration has made reforming the social security a high-priority issue in its agenda, although it ruled out outright privatisation along the lines of the 1981 Chilean reform.[101] As contribution rates are already high, and given the present budget constraint in Mexico, improving the system, and eventually widening its coverage, will have to start with a more efficient use of existing resources. As regards in particular health services, the government's objective is to improve the co-ordination between the social security institutes and the public health system and to make it more market oriented by contracting out a number of services – such as housekeeping functions, certain medical exams, and even family doctors – and decentralising administration and premia-collection, while also offering customers the option to choose among different plans.[102]

V. Meeting basic needs

Overview

For Mexico to reap fully the benefits of market signals and of its integration into the world economy, a sustained effort is needed to bring the levels of education and health more into line with the rest of the OECD and to improve income distribution. Moreover, to the extent that the Chiapas upheaval was due to social inequalities and contributed to capital outflows during 1994, it underscored the high costs of social unrest for a country, such as Mexico, that is dependent on external capital and, therefore, vulnerable to changes in international investors' sentiment. Combining macroeconomic stability with wide-ranging structural reforms, such as those discussed above, is the best long-term strategy to increase living standards in a durable manner.

Such a strategy may not, however, suffice to deal with the problem of poverty. A salient feature of poverty is that it tends to be self-perpetuating inasmuch as the health status and the educational achievements – and hence the earning capacities – of both the poor and their children are worse than for the rest of the population. Breaking the vicious circle of being poor thus calls for special policies, especially for the extremely poor.[103] Some recent reforms, such as those of agricultural support and land tenure as well as those aimed at upgrading skills and competences in the labour force, will have a direct beneficial impact on the neediest in the population. At the same time, other policies may have significant adjustment costs in the short run, making it necessary to alleviate them through some sort of counter-vailing measures.

Although poverty had been reduced during the 1970s, a significant part of the Mexican population was living in precarious conditions at the onset of the 1982 debt crisis. The situation worsened during the subsequent adjustment period and in 1993, after four years of expansion, GDP per capita in constant dollar terms was still below its 1982 level. Despite the policy efforts made to increase public spending on social development and improve targeting and effectiveness of the delivery system, disparities in income and living conditions, both between segments of the population and between regions, remain disturbingly large. The current crisis is likely to aggravate the state of the poor, and the stabilisation programme included short-term measures to meet some of their most pressing needs. Looking further ahead, however, the need persists for a coherent set of policies to exploit the potentially positive and mutually reinforcing links between income distribution, human capital development and economic growth.[104]

The present chapter addresses some key issues pertaining to poverty. First, it describes socio-economic conditions in Mexico in an attempt to evaluate the extent of poverty, pointing to the most important problems and the factors behind these.[105] Second, it reviews the government's strategy to help the poor, focusing in particular on recent efforts aimed at refining the targeting of social programmes and on the new administration's plans to further widen access to social services and improve their quality. Finally, this part examines what remains to be done, in particular in the case of health care.

Poverty and income distribution in Mexico

While measuring poverty is far from straightforward, efficient targeting of public intervention in the fight against poverty critically hinges on defining a threshhold dividing recipients from non-recipients, especially because the poor do not constitute a homogeneous group. When poverty is measured in income terms, such a threshhold can be determined either as the monetary income needed to acquire a set basket of basic goods, primarily food, or in relation to the median income of the population. However, in most developing countries, no income poverty line is defined for policy purposes. Some proxy for poverty is used instead to establish eligibility, and in such a case there are two alternatives. One is a formal definition of poverty in terms of access to basic services and availability of certain consumer durables, which is then tested through regular interviews. A more common, though probably less accurate, approach is to concentrate spending in certain geographical areas or to set benefits in such a way as to discourage the non-poor from claiming them – e.g. setting very low wages in public work programmes or distributing in-kind benefits of inferior quality

Mexico relies to a large extent on the latter approach, although for certain programmes eligibility is defined in relation to the minimum wage.

Estimates of the extent of poverty in Mexico differ according to the chosen methodology. Extreme poverty was estimated at 4 to 10 per cent of the population in 1989, while measures of the incidence of moderate poverty range from 20 to 70 per cent of the population, in that year (Table 21).[106] A recent joint study by the UN Economic Commission for Latin America and the Mexican Statistical Institute (INEGI), based on a common measurement of the poverty line, gives some indication of the evolution of poverty after 1984. The share of the extremely poor in the total population remained virtually unchanged, although the absolute number increased over time (Figure 16). But the period covers two very different sub-periods: in the immediate adjustment phase, from 1984 to 1989, both the number and the share of people in absolute poverty increased; then, during the 1989-92 upswing, there was a slight reduction in poverty. In 1992, 13.6 million people were estimated to be living in conditions of extreme

Table 21. **Different estimates of the extent of poverty in Mexico**[1]

	Poverty line (US$)	Income[2]			Consumption[3]		
		Head-count as per cent of population					
		1984	1989	t-stat	1984	1989	t-stat
Extreme poverty							
Psach. *et al.* (1993)	34.20	2.8	4.0	3.78[4]	3.6	3.5	−0.40
Levy (1991)	50.61	8.0	8.1	0.10	10.2	9.2	−2.08[4]
CEPAL (1990)	56.49	10.5	10.3	−0.31	12.7	11.4	−2.22[4]
Moderate poverty							
Psach. *et al.* (1993)	68.50	16.5	14.8	−2.70[4]	19.5	17.0	−3.68[4]
Szekely (1993)	75.30	19.0	17.9	−1.70	23.2	20.5	−3.75[4]
CEPAL (1990)	108.63	35.8	32.1	−4.50[4]	39.3	35.7	−4.29[4]
Hernandez-Laos (1990)	141.58	47.5	44.0	−4.07[4]	53.1	48.0	−5.93[4]
Levy (1991)	211.95	65.2	62.7	−2.97[4]	70.4	66.7	−4.61[4]
Hernandez-Laos (1990)	238.83	69.5	67.9	−2.05[4]	74.9	71.4	−4.53[4]

1. Poverty lines are per person per quarter in June 1984 prices. Poverty lines were converted to US dollar using the average free exchange rate for 1984 of 185.19 pesos/dollar.
2. Based on quarterly household monetary plus non-monetary income; per capita income was obtained by conversion into adult equivalent units in June 1984 pesos.
3. Based on quarterly household monetary plus non-monetary consumption; per capita consumption was obtained by conversion into adult equivalent units in June 1984 pesos.
4. Indicates that the difference between the 1984 and 1989 estimates is statistically significant at the 5 per cent level.
Source: Lustig, N. and A. Mitchell (1994), "Poverty in Times of Austerity: Mexico in the 1980s", mimeo, presented to the XIII Latin American Meetings of the Econometrics Society, Caracas, 2-5 August.

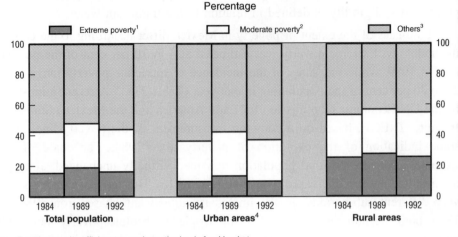

Figure 16. **THE EVOLUTION OF POVERTY SINCE 1984**
Percentage

1. Total income insufficient to purchase the basic food basket.
2. Total income below twice the cost of the basic food basket.
3. Total income above twice the cost of the basic food basket.
4. Municipalities with population larger than 15 000.
Source: CEPAL/INEGI (1993), *Informe sobre la magnitud y evolución de la pobreza en México, 1984-1992.*

poverty. Of these, about 9 million lived in rural areas, where more than half of the population survives on a monetary income which is less than twice the cost of the basic food basket. However, because of the extent of production for own consumption in these areas, evaluations based on monetary income may lead to an overestimation of the problem. Also, many of the benefits provided by poverty alleviation measures do not show up in income, so that other indicators must be considered.

Income has traditionally been more unevenly distributed in Mexico than in the rest of the OECD, with the exception of Turkey (Table 22). During most of the 1980s, high and unpredictable inflation and the difficult transition towards a competitive, free-market economy combined to produce an increase in income inequality, while real per capita income fell by 15 per cent between 1981 and 1988. The evolution in the early 1990s, as shown by the results of the INEGI household income survey for 1989 and 1992 (years for which comparable data are available), is less clear (Table 23):

Table 22. **Income distribution and poverty in selected countries**

	Ratio of income of highest quintile to lowest quintile		Percentage of poor [1]	
Mexico	1984	13.6	1986	51.0
United States	1985	8.9	1986	17.7
Canada	1987	7.1	1987	11.5
Turkey	1987	9.1	1987	25.0
Brazil	1989	32.1	1981	43.0
Korea	1988	5.7	1980	9.8

1. Percentage of people with incomes below the poverty line, defined as: half of the median income for the United States and Canada; twice the cost of basic food basket for Mexico and Brazil; twice the minimum wage for Turkey. No formal threshold indicated for Korea.

Source: OECD (1995), *Economic Survey of Turkey*; Blackburn, M. (1994), "International Comparisons of Poverty", *American Economic Review*, Vol. 84, No. 2; Sakong, I. (1993), *Korea in the World Economy*, Institute for International Economics; World Bank (1994), *World Development Report*, Oxford University Press.

Table 23. **Distribution of household income [1]**

	1992		1989	
	Percentage	Cumulative percentage	Percentage	Cumulative percentage
Household deciles				
I	1.6	1.6	1.6	1.6
II	2.7	4.3	2.8	4.4
III	3.7	8.0	3.7	8.1
IV	4.7	12.7	4.7	12.9
V	5.7	18.4	5.9	18.8
VI	7.1	25.5	7.3	26.1
VII	8.9	34.4	9.0	35.0
VIII	11.4	45.8	11.4	46.5
IX	16.0	61.8	15.6	62.1
X	38.2	100.0	37.9	100.0
Total	100.0	–	100.0	–
Gini coefficient [2]				
Total	0.475		0.469	
Monetary income	0.509		0.489	
Non-monetary income	0.540		0.592	
For deciles I to IX only	0.410		0.406	

1. Average household income per quarter in third quarter 1992, current new pesos. Income includes monetary receipts (job remuneration, business rents, property rents, current transfers received and other incomes) and non-monetary (auto consumption, payments in kind, gifts received, and household rent estimations).
2. Gini coefficients on a per capita income basis would be higher, revealing a more unequal distribution, because household size is on average higher in low-income families.

Source: INEGI and OECD calculations based on the results of the INEGI, Income and Expenditure Survey of Households (*Encuesta Nacional de Ingresos y Gastos de los Hogares*), third quarter 1989, and third quarter 1992.

Table 24. **Social indicators: Mexico in comparative perspective**

1990 unless otherwise stated

Indicator	Mexico 1980	Mexico 1990	United States	Canada	Spain	Portugal	Turkey	Brazil
Crude birth rate (births per thousand population)	31.9	30.0[1]	16.6	15.2	10.2	11.8	26.1[2]	26.7[1]
Crude death rate (deaths per thousand population)	6.6	5.5	8.6	7.2	8.5	10.4	7.5[2]	7.4
Percentage of deaths caused by infectious disease	13.7	9.7	1.4[2]	0.7	1.1[2]	0.8[3]	–	6.0[4]
Life expectancy at birth (years)	66	70	76	77	77	74	65	66
Infant mortality (deaths per thousand births)	53.1	37.0	8.9	6.8	7.8	10.8	56.5	59.0
Fertility rate	4.7	3.3	1.9	1.8	1.5	1.6	3.5	3.3
Literates (per cent of population, 15 years old and older)	83	88	99	99	98	85	81	81
Years of education (people 15 years old and older)	4.9	4.7	12.3	12.1	6.8	6.0	3.5	3.9
Education enrolment (per cent of the population of schooling age)	30	38	100	98	54	48	28	31
Calorie consumption, per capita per day	2 803	3 062	3 600	–	–	–	3 196	2 730
Percentage of households with:								
Piped water	66	81	100	100	100	92	84	86
Sewerage connection	51	63	99	99	96	–	–	78
Electricity	75	75	100	100	95	78	57	79
Owner-occupied house	68		64	60	69	–	–	–
Passenger cars per thousand population	61	65	568	469	307	260	29	104
Telephones per thousand population	72	66	545	577	323	241	123	63
Television sets per thousand population	108	139	814	626	389	176	174	213

1. 1988, estimate.
2. 1989.
3. 1991.
4. 1987.

Source: OECD; UNDP, *World Human Development Report;* United Nations, *Demographic Yearbook;* CEPAL, *Anuario Estadistico de America Latina y el Caribe;* World Bank, *World Development Report;* U.S. Department of Commerce, *Statistical Abstract of the United States;* Instituto Nacional de Estadistica (Spain); Statistics Canada, *Canada Yearbook.*

- the overall deterioration in income distribution has halted, as evidenced by the stable Gini coefficient;
- the three lower deciles of the population experienced little change, their cumulated share in total income remaining stable at around 8 per cent;
- middle-income categories (deciles V to VII) have experienced a deterioration of their relative position; and
- the top 20 per cent of households have seen a minor improvement.

Hence, three years of lower inflation and positive economic growth benefited the highest income categories, while the poorest households were left relatively unaffected.

An alternative method for assessing the extent of poverty is through social indicators. In many cases, there is a significant correlation between dwelling conditions – defined in terms of access to basic services such as electricity, sewerage or pipe water – and possession of household durables, on the one hand, and income levels, on the other. Nonetheless, this is not always the case: it has been noted in many countries that large sections of the population might enjoy continued access to basic services, albeit of lower quality, while their income falls below the poverty line. Inversely, new segments of the population may gain access to basic services even if their income remains well below the poverty threshold. Table 24 compares Mexico with its two NAFTA partners, three Southern European countries and Brazil. It suggests that significant and encouraging improvements occurred in the 1980s, despite deep cuts in social spending, but on many accounts living conditions for most Mexicans remain worse than in the rest of the OECD.[107]

Poverty: causes and manifestations

Extreme poverty continues to be essentially a rural phenomenon, and Southern states, where agriculture accounts for the greatest share of economic activity, are also the poorest ones. This reflects many factors. The development strategy chosen in Mexico in the post-war era placed a heavy burden on the agricultural sector to achieve the goal of rapid industrialisation. A host of price controls often depressed rural income, with prices well below those prevailing on the international market. Nor was public intervention aimed at supporting consumption by poor households of basic foodstuff (*e.g.* tortillas) particularly successful, as the benefits were frequently appropriated by producers, rather than reaching final consumers (Appendini, 1992). The Salinas administration introduced sweeping reforms in the agriculture area that are expected to contribute in the long run to reducing poverty in rural regions, but transition costs may be considerable (see Part IV).

In urban areas, poverty is usually associated with participation in the informal sector. Since the 1960s, the rural poor have increasingly responded to hardships by migrating, either to urban areas – and to the Greater Mexico City area in particular – or to the United States.[108] As labour force growth started overtaking job creation in the formal sector, many workers with no (or little) schooling found employment and a source of subsistence in informal activities, characterised by low productivity, unstable terms of employment and scarce coverage by most labour and social security legislation provisions. A new shock to rural employment is expected from liberalisation measures (Levy and van Weijnberger, 1994), thus making it imperative to tackle problems of the informal sector to improve the living conditions of the urban poor. Apart from the impact of general economic conditions on the creation of jobs in the formal sector, potential poverty-reducing effects in urban areas could be achieved by policies that deregulate formal-sector activities, hence increasing demand for labour (or wages) in microenterprises (Ozorio de Almeida *et al.*, 1994). Programmes to upskill the work force would also facilitate mobility of workers from the informal to the formal sector (see Part IV).

Ethnicity also represents a significant determinant of the probability of being poor: people in more indigenous municipalities live in poorer socio-economic conditions than those in less indigenous ones. Moreover, due to unequal access to schooling, health care and social services more generally, indigenous Mexicans tend to be locked into poor regions or low-wage sectors. This, however, is not sufficient *per se* to explain the width of the earning differentials. Running two separate wage equations – one for the "indigenous" population and the other for the "non-indigenous" one – Patrinos (1994) finds that almost half of the wage difference between indigenous and non-indigenous workers remains unexplained after taking into account such characteristics as education, experience and other control variables. Thus, historical factors, regional economic considerations and discrimination against indigenous people seem to have a significant effect in explaining the extent of poverty, in particular in rural areas. Nevertheless, it is important to remember that in Mexico, the definition of "indigenous" is closely related to linguistic characteristics which limit the access of indigenous people to the labour market.

Poverty is generally associated with low education achievements and poor health conditions. Although aggregate indicators of education attainments have registered rapid improvements after 1988, reflecting intensified government efforts, the picture remains disquieting and regional disparities are still wide.[109] The completion rate at the primary level – measured by the number of students completing the cycle in relation to the flow that entered it six years earlier – was 61 per cent for the 1989-94 cohort (up from 50 per cent in the early 1980s and 55 per cent at the end of the previous decade); in Chiapas, the poorest state, it was only 34 per cent (Table 25). Such a low completion rate, which means that student progress is either slowed down or interrupted, can be attributed to several structural shortcomings, particularly acute in indigenous regions and low-income urban suburbs. In rural areas, schools are often "incomplete" (not offering all six grades) or "single class" (where one teacher teaches all grades); equipment is insufficient; geographical isolation makes it difficult for both teachers and children to reach the school; poor nutrition hinders the students' cognitive skills. In

Table 25. **Education indicators: primary school level, 1993-94**

	Dropout rate	Repetition rate[1]	Terminal efficiency[2]
National average	3.6	8.3	61.1
Rich states			
Federal District	0.3	4.8	85.1
Aguascalientes	0.5	6.1	76.5
Poor states			
Chiapas	7.6	13.3	33.7
Guerrero	9.6	13.1	41.2
Oaxaca	4.5	14.2	49.7

1. 1992-93.
2. Ratio of the number of students finishing primary schooling in year 1993-94 to the number of students entering first grade in school year 1987-88.
Source: Salinas de Gortari, C. (1994), *Sexto Informe de Gobierno*, and data provided by national authorities.

Figure 17. **MORTALITY RATES BY REGIONS**

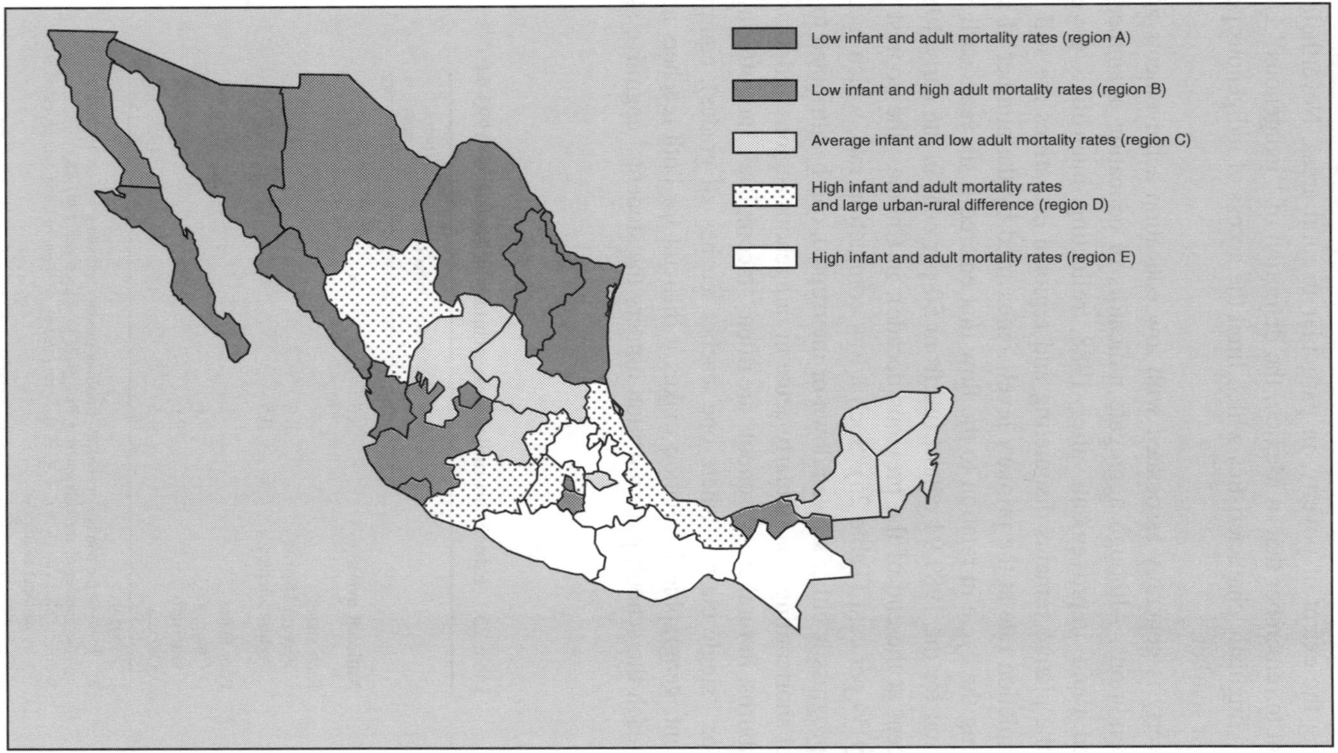
Low infant and adult mortality rates (region A)
Low infant and high adult mortality rates (region B)
Average infant and low adult mortality rates (region C)
High infant and adult mortality rates and large urban-rural difference (region D)
High infant and adult mortality rates (region E)

Source: Frenk, J., R. Lozano et M. Gonzales-Black (1994), *Economía y salud*, FUNSALUD, Mexico City.

addition, in both rural and urban areas there is strong pressure on children from low-income families to start working at an early age, causing absenteeism – and hence poor results – or high drop-out rates.

Aggregate Mexican health statistics paint the picture of an upper middle income developing country, with moderate mortality and low malnutrition rates (World Bank, 1994). Over the past decades, a major fertility and epidemiological transition has taken place, with declines in both the birth and death rates. But these figures hide widespread disparity among different income classes and among regions. Certain parts of the country have health statistics that are close to OECD averages, while other regions have seen only a relatively small improvement in their health status and resemble the poor South Asian countries. The Mexican Foundation of Health divides the country into five regions based on infant and adult mortality rates (Figure 17). The region with the best health status is made up of eight states located to the north of Mexico City and the Federal District. The worst health statistics are found in the Southern region – the five states with the lowest per capita income and with larger than average indigenous populations (Table 26). A significant part of the difference in mortality among states reflects differences in the incidence of infectious diseases, these in turn being explained by differences in education and sanitary conditions.

Table 26. **Health indicators**

	Number of states	Total population (millions)	Mortality rate		Percentage of deaths due to infectious disease
			Infant	Adult	
National average	32[1]	85.6	31.9	3.3	12.2
Mortality region A	9[1]	22.2	22.4	2.9	8.4
B	6	13.4	27.5	3.3	10.0
C	7	10.9	37.3	3.3	13.4
D	5	23.4	33.4	3.4	12.5
E	5	15.7	43.3	3.9	19.0

1. Including Mexico City (Federal District). For the states included in each region, see Annex Table A4.
Source: OECD calculations based on data provided by national authorities.

Poverty alleviation: the National Solidarity Programme

Objectives, organisation and financing

The National Solidarity strategy (Solidaridad), an umbrella organisation in charge of co-ordinating health, nutrition, education, infrastructure, and productive projects, was the centre-piece of the Salinas government's initiative to improve living conditions for the poor. Before Solidaridad was put in place in 1988, subsidies for poverty relief had been insufficient (when at all) targeted, giving rise to both horizontal and vertical inequalities. As similar programmes implemented in Latin America (Bolivia and Chile) and elsewhere (Senegal and Zambia), it was created to alleviate the impact on the poor of the reduction of income and employment caused by the debt crisis and the adjustment measures taken to lay the basis for renewed growth.[110] Solidarity aims at providing a safety net for the weakest social segments, improving efficiency and redistributive impact of social spending through better targeting. At the same time, as a demand-based social fund, it encourages the active participation of beneficiaries both in selecting and implementing the projects.

When it started, Solidarity depended on the Programming and Budgeting Ministry, there being no additional administrative structure. In 1992, it was transferred to the newly-created Ministry of Social Development (Secretaria de Desarrollo Social, SEDESOL). The overall budget-making responsibilities are given to the Treasury, which allocates funds to SEDESOL in a single federal budget line (*Ramo 26*). SEDESOL in turn allocates the money among states, which then provided additional revenues according to the Social Development Agreements, signed by each state with the Ministry.[111] Qualifying municipalities are then designated by state governments. At the local level, projects are proposed by community- or neighbourhood-based committees in response to residents' expressed preferences; the responsibility for overseeing project implementation is borne by these committees (Figure 18).

Overall public spending on social development (health, education, urban development, etc.) has increased substantially since 1988, to about 10 per cent of GDP in 1993 and 1994, representing more than 50 per cent of the total programmed expenditure in the government budget (Table 27). Solidarity budget also increased significantly, more than doubling since 1988 to 0.7 per cent of GDP. Besides its targeting elements, what puts Solidarity apart from the rest of

Figure 18. **THE ORGANISATION OF SOLIDARITY**

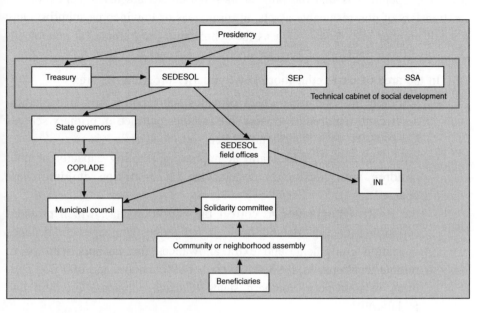

Note: SEDESOL: Ministry of Social Development;
SEP: Ministry of Public Education;
SSA: Ministry of Health and Welfare;
COPLADE: Planning Committee for State Development;
INI: National Indigenous Institute.
Source: OECD.

Table 27. **Social and Solidarity spending**

Billions of current pesos and percentages

	1989	1990	1991	1992	1993	1994
Total Solidarity spending	3.09	6.50	10.23	13.95	16.46	18.41
of which:						
Social Development Agreements	1.64	3.28	5.19	6.99	8.26	9.23
Solidarity for Social Welfare	0.97	1.87	3.16	4.21	5.22	6.31
Solidarity for Production	0.17	0.88	0.99	1.56	1.87	1.65
Basic infrastructure	0.31	0.47	0.89	1.19	1.11	1.22
Solidarity spending (as a share of GDP)	(0.61)	(0.95)	(1.18)	(1.37)	(1.48)	(1.48)
Public spending on social development[1]	31.33	44.42	66.72	88.01	106.99	–
Public spending on social development (as a share of GDP)	(6.18)	(6.49)	(7.70)	(8.64)	(9.59)	–
Solidarity spending (as a share of public spending on social development)	(9.86)	(14.63)	(15.33)	(15.85)	(15.38)	–

1. Includes education, health care, regional and urban development.
Source: Salinas de Gortari, C. (1994), *Sexto Informe de Gobierno*.

the social spending is that the bulk of its programmes are investment projects, *i.e.* transfers of non-resaleable assets, in rural areas or low income suburbs. Only a small number of projects, such as the scholarship programme for schoolchildren, qualify as transfers of current income (see Annex I, Table A3).

In the area of basic education, key Solidarity programmes are:

–   Children in Solidarity, which provides scholarships and free medical services to children of low-income families enrolled in primary schools (in 1993-94, over 1 million children participated);
–   school breakfasts, which aim at improving learning capacity of poor children with nutritional deficiencies (1.25 million children were covered);
–   the PARE (Programme to correct the education lag), which provides supporting material, notably books in indigenous languages and distance education equipment, and extra allowances for teachers who go to remote locations; in 1993, it covered 9 000 schools and 600 000 children, in four poor Southern states (Oaxaca, Chiapas, Guerrero and Hidalgo);[112]
–   Schools in Solidarity, which supports backward schools (other than those covered by PARE) in several states, contributing to infrastructure development; the programme, which started in 1991-92, is estimated to have covered about 3 500 schools and 330 000 children by 1994.

An evaluation of results

Compared with similar programmes in other developing countries, Solidarity is far bigger in size and far wider in scope, so that assessing what it has achieved is correspondingly more difficult. Moreover, its objectives are complex and under binding budget constraints possibly at cross-purpose. Although it is difficult to judge whether it has been cost effective, there can be no doubt that, if only because of its sheer size, the programme has had a major impact on the living conditions of many Mexicans, through infrastructure projects such as schools, rural clinics, and electricity connections.[113] By improving the range and quality of the services to which people have access, it put in place some necessary conditions for raising income levels in the medium-term. As for jobs created by Solidarity enterprises, most have been temporary; only 85 000 permanent jobs were created in 9 210 Solidarity enterprises in the 3 years to November 1994.[114]

Solidarity is a multi-pronged programme, the effects of which will only become evident as time passes. It would be unwise to dismiss it simply because its achievements, after only a few years of implementation, are not reflected in a reduction of the number of people under the poverty line. The main difference between Solidaridad and public social spending in general resides in the way it is targeted. However, formal targeting mechanisms have only been used for two food subsidy programmes (Tortivales and Liconsa), which are part of Solidarity but are independently run by CONASUPO (Grosh, 1994).[115] In both cases, participation is supposed to be limited to families whose income is less than twice the minimum wage, and relatively simple means tests are carried out by social workers. Neighbourhood-level targeting is also used, distributing food through shops that are located in poor areas, therefore introducing a disincentive for the non-poor to misuse these programmes. Results appear to have been satisfactory, in that benefits have accrued mainly to targeted groups and leakages have been minimal. The main limitation of such food subsidy programmes has been that they have primarily benefited the urban poor (but not necessarily the poorest among them), while having a more limited impact in rural areas.[116]

An alternative mechanism to ensure targeting and one that has been increasingly used in the context of Solidarity is to have the recipients select the projects. The demand-driven nature of the programme may well have restored confidence and self-esteem among its beneficiaries. Demand-driven targeting, however, may not always be the most appropriate: the poorest are usually not the most vocal segments of the population, and lack of information may lead them to imperfect choices concerning the projects they desire from Solidarity. This is why it is argued that "centrally implemented public works programme(s) are better suited for rapid, mass-scale targeting of the poorest sectors".[117] While most observers consider that Solidarity deconcentrated – rather than decentralised – administration, they also point out that the programme can strengthen political actors (such as Non-Governmental Organisations, NGOs) that may, in the longer term, push for decentralisation and democratisation.[118] The experience of other countries, such as Bolivia, with demand-driven social funds shows that their success in motivating participation and ensuring transparency partly depends on the role played by NGOs; conversely, only political opening will allow NGOs to really exert a voice in the management of Solidarity's finance. This is especially relevant for Mexico where the more vocal among the poor have traditionally been those linked to the ruling party, and not necessarily the poorest among them.

The road ahead: reforming the health care system and improving social policies

Building up human capital is a lengthy process, and it is now widely recognised that learning is facilitated by good health, which in turn is helped when essential nutrients are available.[119] Among Solidarity's various programmes, those like Children in Solidarity and the school breakfast package that combine teaching and the provision of essential nutrients and health care deserve a special mention. The new administration intends to continue and extend the national system of Family Integral Development (DIF), which caters for families with young children (the most vulnerable population) in 500 priority municipalities by providing school breakfasts, a food basket, health services, information on nutrition and sanitary habits and family planning. The long-term objective is to expand the delivery of school breakfasts fourfold over five years, to serve 5 million children. Changes in the delivery system are under study to facilitate access to remote rural areas. To the extent that the programme succeeds in improving health, education and family planning among the rural poor, it may also prove to be the best way to promote a further slowdown in population growth, which is much less marked in rural than in urban areas.

Access to medical services mirrors the differences in income throughout the country: certain groups and areas have access to extremely modern health care at a subsidised cost, while others are isolated from even the most basic health care. The government provides universal health care with the goal of making services available to those who are not covered by social security and who cannot afford private health care – in principle, about a third of the population. In reality, a significant percentage of the population is not covered by any health service due to their economic situation and geographic isolation. On the other hand, there is often overlap in both coverage and services between the many different health programmes that form the national health system. The access to health facilities differs greatly across regions, as well as between urban and rural areas. As a general rule, there are more medical personnel and equipment in rich states than in poor; in capital cities than in other cities; in urban areas than in rural ones; and in the Federal District relative to anywhere else.[120] In the case of public health facilities, the geographical distribution is more equitable than for the private or the social security systems – although there is still a bias in favour of the Federal District. For low-income people in rural areas, there are significant barriers to the use of public health clinics, such as travel time, transportation expenses, waiting time and, at least for the poorest, the fee charged (even though it is low in absolute terms).

In terms of public resources spent on health care, it is clear that the distribution is not equitable: the social security sector spends approximately four times as much as the public health system, even if about half of the population is not covered by any social security plan.[121] There are also important problems of misallocation of resources, as shown by the significant proportion of doctors or nurses reporting that they are unemployed (or underemployed) in large cities, while there may be lack of staff in smaller and poorer communities. One of the major complaints about the public health sector is thus the poor quality and lack of attention of government-run facilities. This is reflected in a relatively high use of private health facilities even among the lower income middle classes, despite the fact that public services are virtually free (Frenk *et al.*, 1994).

Because poor health is both a cause and an effect of poverty, improving the population's health status and increasing access to basic health care has been an integral element of the government anti-poverty plan. Over the last few years, progress has been made in improving the quality of services and extending coverage to less favoured groups, while new infrastructure has been built. Some financing and organisational reforms were also implemented. Regarding medical services in poor communities, an agreement was signed by Solidaridad and IMSS (the Social Security Institute) to supply health care, education and community services and to develop infrastructure, following an integrated approach. Important results were achieved with various initiatives promoting vaccination in rural areas, nutrition education and the use of purified water. Family planning was also extended in this context.

As part of its medium-term goal to reduce poverty, the new government is committed to continue improving the provision of preventive and curative health care. Among stated objectives, attention to the most vulnerable groups and extension of coverage are foremost (Mexico, 1995). Given the resource constraint imposed by the economic emergency, at least in the short run, progress is to be achieved largely through improved efficiency. As reported in the National Development Plan, several key reforms are being studied, affecting both the organisation of the national health service and the range of services that are offered:

- merge the different social security sectors into IMSS, to consolidate medical facilities, reduce double coverage of members, and obtain savings on administrative costs;
- further decentralise public health services, transferring more resources and functions to states;
- set a basic health package that defines the minimum level of medical care that each citizen is entitled to. The government would ensure that all low-income families have access to it; and
- reinforce preventive actions targeted at the most vulnerable groups.

VI.   Conclusions

The Mexican economy has been in the process of costly adjustment since the currency crisis erupted in December 1994. The general climate of uncertainty persisted despite the January stabilisation programme and the initial package of international financial support. The volatility in financial and foreign exchange markets began to diminish only in late March in the wake of the announcement of the more stringent set of stabilisation measures and the enhanced international financial support. By then the peso had fallen by 50 per cent against the dollar from its pre-crisis level, and short-term interest rates were hovering around 80 per cent. By July, there were ample signs of improved market confidence. The peso had recovered 20 per cent from its trough, and interest rates were close to 40 per cent. The stock market had recovered the losses recorded since the start of the year. Sharply falling domestic absorption and surging exports helped reduce the current account deficit to US$1.2 billion in the first quarter of 1995, from US$6.7 billion a year earlier. By mid-July, the government had redeemed over two-thirds of the outstanding stock of Tesobonos. The large currency deprecia- tion, an increase in the VAT rate, and adjustment in public prices pushed domes- tic inflation to a peak monthly rate of 8 per cent in April. But inflation has been falling rapidly since then, and signs are emerging that point to sharp labour market adjustment. Also, some needed adjustments are occurring in the banking sector, helped by the government's support measures to restructure loan portfo- lios and legal reforms to attract new capital.

The crisis had multiple causes, and it would be futile to attempt to establish the relative importance of each. With the benefit of hindsight, however, it is possible to understand how the crisis occurred and was amplified. The ground was prepared by a configuration of economic conditions which resulted largely from the policies pursued in the past several years. The monetary policy approach, based essentially on pegging the peso to the US dollar, succeeded in bringing down inflation to a single digit level. Disinflation was accompanied by large capital inflows and a strong real appreciation of the peso. Fiscal consolidation up to 1992 and sterilisation of such inflows tended to dampen the expansion of domestic spending. However, the relaxation of the fiscal policy stance and a rapid growth of loans by government-owned development banks since 1993 contributed to the recovery of domestic demand and imports in 1994. Activity was also stimulated by a rapid expansion of credit to the private sector by commercial banks, although lending growth decelerated in the course of 1994, and was substantially lower on average than a year earlier. Competition for market shares (mainly among small and medium sized banks) in the wake of financial liberalisation also contributed to a significant deterioration in the quality of their loans. All of these factors combined to produce a large and widening current account deficit, a mirror image of national saving insufficient to finance investment. At the same time, up to the first quarter of 1994, there were substantial capital inflows, mainly of a short term nature. While it is normal for a country like Mexico to rely on foreign capital to meet part of its investment needs, the scale of such financing and heavy reliance on short-term capital made the situation highly susceptible to changes in investors' perceptions.

Against this backdrop, rising US interest rates reduced the relative attractiveness of emerging markets generally, and a series of political disturbances in Mexico during 1994 undermined investors' confidence. In the wake of the Chiapas uprising in January, the assassination in March of the leading presidential candidate precipitated a first wave of capital flight; the peso fell to the lower limit of the exchange rate band; and the intervention to defend the peso led to a large loss of foreign reserves. Reserves thereafter remained broadly unchanged up to November despite further political disturbances, although this result was partly achieved through the issue of large volumes of dollar-indexed securities (Tesobonos). The announcement of the initial budget for 1995 which did not imply an increase in public saving may have been a disappointment to investors. With the relapse of the situation in Chiapas in early December, the peso came under renewed downward pressure. The new government announced a widening of the fluctuation band of the peso, allowing a 15 per cent devaluation; two days later, under continued selling pressure it chose to float the currency.

The role of monetary policy in this episode has been a subject of active debate. Although money-market interest rates were increased significantly in

March 1994 in the initial response to the selling pressure on the peso, bank loans continued to grow at high, albeit decelerating, rates. The overall strategy was aimed at avoiding exclusive reliance on monetary tightening. In particular, an exchange-rate depreciation within the fluctuation band was combined with heavy use of foreign exchange intervention, as well as increased supplies of Tesobonos, to try to relieve pressures on the market and avoid steeper increases in domestic interest rates. This choice of strategy reflected the background against which decisions had to be made: the authorities were reluctant to raise interest rates more sharply for the fear that such a decision might aggravate the problem of bad loans in the banking sector, and the alternative policy of devaluing or floating the peso earlier in 1994, an election year, would have been politically difficult. The course adopted also reflected an assessment that the pressures on the exchange rate were transitory, as had been the case when similar measures were taken in November 1993 (prior to approval of NAFTA). However, when the shocks in 1994 proved to be persistent, the strategy adopted became unsustainable.

The scale of the crisis was probably amplified by a number of factors. Under the assumption that the pressures against the exchange rate would be short-lived, the authorities intervened in the foreign exchange market to maintain the peso within its band. This weakened their foreign reserve position, thereby constraining their capacity to support the currency when turbulence persisted. In this context, the accumulated stock of Tesobonos liabilities, built up earlier in the year while defending the peso, turned out to be a major weakness. Delays in announcing the devaluation and the related stabilisation package – inevitable given the importance attached to the Pacto framework in which these decisions were taken – aggravated the general climate of uncertainty. This was compounded by perceptions of insufficient communications with financial markets in the initial devaluation announcement. Once confidence was lost, market reactions took on a partly self-fulfilling character as loss of liquidity in Mexican financial markets contributed to fears that the government would be unable to meet its short-term obligations. In retrospect, it seems that the deepening of the crisis might have been reduced, or even avoided, had a more appropriate policy mix been adopted earlier in 1994 – one more suited to deal with permanent shocks rather than temporary ones. Then perhaps the resultant adjustment process would have been less traumatic than the one that is now under way.

The strong policy measures put in place in two steps (January and March) should help restore balance in the economy. The tight budget position and restrictive monetary policy are exerting deflationary forces on domestic spending, while Mexican exporters are making good use of the improved international competitive position. With the current account likely to be broadly in balance and the currently-available short-term financing facilities, the authorities should be able to meet the external liabilities that fall due in 1995. As the year progresses, it will become increasingly important to re-establish a sustainable pattern of voluntary financing from international capital markets. In this regard, recent international bond issues by the Mexican government and public institutions are encouraging steps.

How long the adjustment is likely to take remains an open question. The government projects that the economy will rebound in the second half of this year. The Secretariat's assessment is that the impact of the stabilisation measures would be more severe and that the recovery of activity is likely to be a more protracted process. This is largely because unwinding the poor balance-sheet positions of banks, companies and households is bound to take some time, as experience in other OECD countries has shown. Although the measures of loan restructuring announced by the government should ease the liquidity problems of the borrowers, it is difficult to envisage a rapid generalised upswing in spending in such a debt-constrained economy. The Secretariat projects output to start recovering around the end of 1995 as the positive effects of expanding exports and falling interest rates permeate the economy.

A key factor underpinning this outlook will be the success of monetary policy in ensuring that the depreciation does not lead to an inflationary spiral. In the short term, progress toward this objective will be helped by the large slack in the economy, the modest response of wages to the pickup of inflation, and the monetary policy commitments that have been adopted for 1995. These commitments involve adhering to announced limits on central bank credit expansion, along with the general goals of promoting stability in the foreign exchange market and resisting higher-than-projected inflation. Provided confidence continues to improve in financial markets, these objectives should be consistent with a further easing of short-term interest rates towards more normal levels as inflation and financial risk premia decline.

Restoration of confidence will, however, depend significantly on establishing a sound medium-term framework for monetary policy that can help to anchor expectations beyond the current year. A return to some form of exchange-rate peg seems unlikely to be feasible in the near future while reserves remain low and inflation well above international levels. In view of these difficulties, and the need to establish some framework that will discipline future policies and help to build credibility, the most promising option might be to move towards an inflation-targeting system, building on recent efforts to make inflation objectives more explicit. Giving primacy to an inflation objective would not preclude a significant role for the exchange rate as a policy indicator. It would require further steps to make the central bank more clearly accountable for meeting the objectives and to enhance its operational independence. Explicit inflation objectives would have to be carefully formulated to avoid being either insufficiently restrictive or unrealistically ambitious. An important priority in adopting a more explicit inflation target would be to develop a clearer system of indicators of inflationary pressures and greater expertise in forecasting such pressures. In this context, improvements are needed in the quality, coverage and timeliness of economic and financial data collected and diffused to the public so as to allow appropriate policy reactions to unfolding events and to facilitate more effective public evaluation of monetary policy actions.

One factor which has complicated monetary policy decisions has been a worsening of the balance-sheet position of a number of banks since financial liberalisation began at the end of the 1980s. The rapid growth of bank lending to the private sector that followed was reinforced by the shift in banks' portfolio due to the correction of the public deficit. As was the case in a number of other countries after financial liberalisation, the expansion of commercial bank credit to the private sector was also accompanied by an increase in bad loans. This experience suggests that the banks' internal control of the quality of loans and the system of supervision were less than satisfactory. Any weakening of the public's trust in financial markets and institutions would also risk hampering the much-needed increase in private savings which are low relative to many of the high-growth economies with comparable income levels. It is, therefore, important that recent efforts to tighten prudential standards and disclosure requirements in the financial sector should be continued, in order to bring the Mexican system into line with international standards.

The sharp increase in government savings embodied in the revised budget for 1995 is an orthodox and appropriate response to the crisis. The underlying financial position of the Mexican government remains sound, as a result of the major efforts to improve the fiscal position up to 1992. Uncertainties about the effects on the budget of structural changes, such as privatisation and decentralisation, make quantitative projections beyond the immediate future impractical for the time being. A clearly articulated medium-term fiscal strategy will need to be developed, which includes not only medium-term fiscal objectives but also an indication of the transition path towards achieving them. To function as a useful instrument of macroeconomic policy and to enhance credibility, the strategy would need to take into account a number of factors, including: low levels of national savings; the effects of the cycle on the budget, so that the underlying structural budget position can be assessed; the timing of the transition from the current tight fiscal stance to a more neutral position in order to avoid providing macroeconomic stimulus at an inappropriate point in the cycle – in this context the size of loans by development banks should also be consistent with the macroeconomic policy stance; and the possible risks and contingent liabilities affecting the budget. These factors together point to the need to maintain a prudent and cautious approach to any change in fiscal policy settings.

There is a clear need for increased spending on infrastructure and social development, but limited room for raising tax rates. Reforms to improve efficiency of both public spending and taxation should form an integral part of the government's medium-term strategy. There is considerable scope for continuing efforts to reallocate resources within the overall budget to enhance the effectiveness of public spending. But in order to make proper assessments of programme effectiveness and efficiency, to identify where real improvements can be made and to monitor progress, more detailed information on the costs of specific activities are needed. In addition, a systematic re-examination of the way the public service operates and the ways in which the incentive structure built into present arrangements affects performance would be necessary in order to make significant improvements in public-sector efficiency. Raising productivity will probably require some shedding of staff unless they can be absorbed into the expanding priority activities. On the revenue side, improving tax collection, as intended by the government, will be key to increasing revenues. The review of taxation that is under way is timely and seems to be appropriately oriented towards broadening the tax base, finding the mix of direct and indirect taxes that would encourage savings, investment and employment, and re-examining the revenue sharing arrangements between the federal government, states and municipalities. At the same time, the roles of different levels of government are being reassessed with a view to providing greater responsibility to states and municipalities in the provision of public services.

The issues raised above point to the usefulness of having a clearly articulated medium-term macroeconomic policy framework in order to guide policy decisions as the current adjustment phase comes to an end. Indeed, such a framework may facilitate the adjustment process by providing reassurance to investors about Mexico's medium-term prospects. Equally important in this context are structural reforms, a pillar of the strategy of the previous as well as the present government.

In many respects, Mexico's record in implementing structural reforms is remarkable. Deep-rooted government interference in economic activities was substantially reduced in less than a decade through the massive sale of State assets, bold reforms in agriculture, the liberalisation of financial markets and a spectacular opening of the economy to international trade, leading to the signing of NAFTA and other trade agreements. Market forces now shape economic activity to a far greater extent than before, and the government did not resort to capital controls or border protection in response to the current crisis. Although there have been social costs in such reforms, further delays in implementing long-due changes would have only made the situation of the poor worse through higher prices, regressive use of public subsidies and overall allocative distortions.

The new administration has reiterated its commitment to the goal of improving the living conditions of the country's poorest. This is reflected in the emphasis on maintaining social spending in the austerity budget this year, the measures that were taken to alleviate the impact of the adjustment on the poor and some of the lines of action described in the National Development Plan of May 1995, the strategy programme of the government for the six-year period that has just begun. Fighting poverty has been high on the Mexican government's agenda for the last several years. Targeted programmes, notably Solidarity, made more effective the delivery of the benefits of public intervention to the neediest and the poorest. Despite the policy efforts made and the increase in financial resources devoted to this purpose, however, poverty remains widespread and income inequality among

121

the highest in the OECD area, the most critical situation being found in some of the rural areas with significant indigenous presence. The new government intends to continue the policies of decentralisation and targeting as well as of putting emphasis on the participation of beneficiaries and the inclusion of more demand-driven elements in the design of policies. In order to enhance further the effectiveness of programmes, however, it is important to increase the transparency of decision-making at the local level and avoid inappropriate political interference. Providing the poor with opportunities and incentives to participate actively in the design of specific policies is important not only as a way of improving their material well-being but also to increase their sense of participation in society.

Despite the impressive list of structural reform measures adopted over the last decade or so there remain many unfinished tasks, and the current crisis unveiled certain weaknesses of past reforms as well as new challenges. It is imperative to increase the momentum of reform and broaden its approach. The emergency programme adopted in early 1995 includes major measures of structural reform, notably plans for a new round of privatisation and deregulation in the areas of ports, railroads, telecommunications, airports, secondary petrochemical and natural gas. While ruling out the possibility of allowing private-sector participation in oil extraction, the government intends to pursue more aggressively the privatisation of non-core PEMEX activities.

The experience of a number of countries convincingly demonstrates that, important as privatisation may be, the largest potential for welfare gains comes from regulatory reforms and the enforcement of competition policy. Some early privatisations, which were carried out without a proper regulatory framework, have yielded limited welfare gains. For example, the largest privatised firm, the telephone company, remains sheltered from competition until 1996, and regulatory uncertainties have plagued the operation of the two formerly State-owned airlines. The recent creation of the Federal Competition Commission is an appropriate step. New laws to liberalise key sectors such as telecoms and natural gas have already been approved, and these are welcome. In the future, however, it will be desirable to establish an appropriate regulatory framework well before the changes in ownership. It is also important to reinforce the existing regulatory authorities, making them independent of political pressures.

Much has to be done to improve the functioning of labour markets. Current legislation regarding employment and social security provisions, where it is enforced, is likely to inhibit mobility between sectors and, more generally, act as a disincentive to the use of labour. Inflexible dismissal procedures and high severance payments raise the cost of labour. In a country with an abundant and fast-growing labour supply, like Mexico, it is important to reduce biases against the use of labour. But modifying existing labour legislation alone would not be sufficient to deal with the problem of trisected labour markets – where a large rural sector coexists with the formal and informal sectors in urban areas – and to foster the creation of higher productivity jobs. Recent achievements and announced programmes to expand the coverage and raise the quality of basic education and, more generally, to upgrade skills and competences need to be continued. Reforming the social security system, as envisaged in the National Development Plan, should be part of the overall approach. Improving the efficiency of the existing system is the first step, to be followed by a widening of its coverage. Various schemes are already in place that provide income support for the jobless, but if dismissal conditions are eased, the need to widen the safety net is bound to increase.

To sum up, the Mexican economy is in the early phase of the adjustment necessitated by the currency crisis. The stabilisation measures adopted, along with the package of international financial assistance, are already having an effect and should be able to bring about a restoration of macroeconomic balance. In parallel, the government has expressed its determination to deepen structural reforms as evidenced by the Constitutional and other legal changes that have been made to prepare the necessary ground. It is necessary to continue with various structural reforms to enhance both efficiency and equity along the lines of the National Development Plan. The combination of sound macroeconomic, structural and social policies is the best route to achieving low inflation and real income convergence with the rest of the OECD.

Notes

1. Here and in the following, depreciation and appreciation of the exchange rate are expressed as the changes in the dollar value of the peso.

2. In 1994, aggregate consumption (private consumption in particular) was growing in line with GDP in contrast to much higher growth in the period 1989-92, when private savings declined steeply in relation to GDP. As there are no appropriation accounts by sectors for Mexico, only indirect measures of private savings are available, and it is impossible to establish a distinction between households and business. The existence of a large informal sector, on which timely data are lacking, also makes analysis of the household sector difficult. Wage-earners registered with the social security institutes account for only about half of total employment; a significant share of non-farm employment, mostly self-employed, is occupied in informal activities. By providing some income to those who lose their jobs in the formal sector of the economy, and thereby playing the role of a safety net, the informal sector typically dampens the impact of shocks on household income.

3. These results are based on an econometric study over the period 1965-92 conducted at the central bank. In this exercise, financial assets include government securities held by the public and gross private sector deposits in commercial banks. Real estate value is not included because of insufficient data. For details, see Buira (1994).

4. Developments in 1993 were very contrasted, with investment in machinery and equipment declining, but construction, including housing, remaining strong.

5. The respective trends of public and private investment over the early 1990s are very much influenced by privatisation. The rapid expansion of private investment in machinery and equipment (some 17 per cent per year on average in 1991-92) reflects to a large extent investments by newly-privatised enterprises, that were previously recorded as public investment. Over the same period, public investment fell by 6.5 per cent per year.

6. Export growth of goods and services in the National Accounts is understated (and lower than what is suggested by the growth of exports of goods and services on a customs basis) because National Accounts are based on 1980 weights, when the share of oil in total exports was much larger, and that of manufactured products correspondingly lower, than in recent years.

7. After a long process of restructuring during the 1980s, the New Zealand economy nearly stagnated until 1991, recovering thereafter. For details on the slow response to structural reform and improved recent performance of that country, see OECD (1993) and (1994), *Economic Survey of New Zealand.*

8. The INEGI Monthly Survey of Industry, that covers developments in large-sized existing firms but excludes in-bond exporting industries ("maquiladoras") and most small enterprises, suggests that layoffs during 1994 were more widespread than indicated by the data on insured workers. However, job creation in newly-established enterprises and in small- and medium-sized firms is not apprehended in the survey sample.

9. The share of the labour force engaged in informal activities has increased since the start of the 1980s to perhaps 35 per cent of the total labour force in 1993, against 25 per cent in 1970. During most of the 1980s, low economic growth was the main factor. After 1988, the shift of employment from industry to the service sector and from large firms to smaller firm has been important; half of the cumulative increase in labour supply over the period is estimated to have gone into the informal sector. Developments in the informal sector can be discerned through the Survey of Microenterprises and the Urban Employment Survey (which reports information on the number of persons employed in firms of 1 to 5 people, persons in short-term occupations and on irregular schedules, those earning subsistence-level incomes, etc.).

10. The Industry Survey conducted by INEGI in 37 urban areas covers mostly large enterprises; for many industrial branches, only a small number of firms are included in the sample. Productivity growth in the large manufacturing sector, already on a rapidly rising trend for several years, accelerated to about 8 per cent in 1994. Calculations based on National Accounts data point to more modest labour productivity gains in the manufacturing sector over the recent period.

11. Experience in other OECD countries, Spain and Portugal in particular after their entry into the EU, suggest that sustained export market share gains can be achieved through structural changes, despite a deterioration in relative competitive position. For details on OECD's competitiveness indicators see Durand et al. (1992).

12. Unless indicated otherwise, merchandise trade excludes imports and exports of the in-bond sector, which are recorded as non-factor services, in accordance with the methodology currently applied for other OECD countries.

13. As there are no official estimates of the breakdown of merchandise trade into volumes and average values since 1992, the data that serve as a basis for the present analysis have been estimated by the OECD Secretariat. Estimates of price changes, based on various indirect indicators, are used to deflate the trade flows. It follows that the evolutions described should be interpreted as indicative of broad trends only.

14. In the early 1990s the main force underpinning capital goods imports was the intense investment effort of previously protected industries seeking to meet increased competition, while export growth remained slow. In 1994, intermediate products imports (around 60 per cent of total merchandise imports) were boosted by the surge in exports. Capital goods account for slightly more than 20 per cent and consumer goods for slightly less; the relative share of the last two items would need to be adjusted to allow for the fact that Mexican statistics classify products such as TV and radio sets and cameras as capital goods – although the adjustment would be marginal since the volume of imports of these goods is still very small.

15. Export market growth is calculated by the OECD Secretariat on the basis of a weighted average of import volumes of manufactured goods in Mexico's main trading partners, with weights based on manufacturing trade flows in 1991. Mexico's export markets, thus defined,

grew by 16.7 per cent in 1994. As a result of NAFTA, Mexican trade within this area intensified. Total exports to the United States increased by 20 per cent in dollar terms, including in-bond industries, while the United States' total imports were rising by 15 per cent. Mexican exports to the rest of the world expanded by 4.3 per cent.

16. The external public debt does not include government securities (such as Cetes and Tesobonos) that are issued on the domestic market and held by non-residents.

17. In 1994, FDI was mainly channelled towards manufacturing and services (including finance) – each accounting for 40 per cent of the total – as well as transport and communications – 8.5 per cent. In the last six years, Mexico was the third largest host country among developing economies for FDI flows (after China and Singapore). In 1994, it received 13 per cent of all FDI channelled to the developing world, and more than 50 per cent of FDI going to Latin America and the Caribbean.

18. The discussion below refers to the public sector financial balance including the Federal government, the social security system, public enterprises under budgetary control (including PEMEX), as well as large entities outside budgetary control. Revenues from privatisation are excluded from the financial balance. As of 1993, financial intermediation by development banks is not recorded in the public sector finances. For the period prior to 1993, the "economic" balance, which according to the Mexican terminology excludes financial intermediation, is used. Debt figures refer to total net debt of the public sector consolidated with Bank of Mexico; in this case, government financial intermediaries (*i.e.* development banks and official trust funds) are included.

19. The primary balance is the financial balance *less* net interest payments.

20. After adjusting for inflation (*i.e.* deducting the portion of the interest payments that constitutes accelerated repayment of the principal), the surplus amounted to 2.9 per cent of GDP in 1992, as in 1991. The adjustment is particularly relevant during high-inflation periods: on the one hand, rapid inflation leads to high nominal interest rates, hence high interest payments to service the public debt; but high inflation also erodes the real value of the government debt. Thus the inflation component of interest payments should be deducted as it corresponds effectively to accelerated repayment (amortisation) of the principal. The "inflation effect" applies to the portion of public debt that is denominated in domestic currency and is not indexed. By 1992, with the slowing of inflation, the size of the corresponding adjustment to the public sector balance had fallen below 1 percentage point of GDP.

21. Data limitations (there are no general government appropriation accounts on a National Accounts basis in Mexico) make it difficult to calculate a cyclically-adjusted budget balance for Mexico according to the methodology applied to most of the other OECD countries.

22. Provisions on income tax cuts and public tariffs were negotiated in the Pacto. Tariffs on rail cargo, airport services, and electricity for industrial use were cut by 10 per cent or more in order to reduce costs for the business sector.

23. See Part V below for a discussion of Solidaridad role.

24. Tesobonos accounted for less than 3 per cent of total government securities held by the public at the end of 1993; the proportion had risen to 55 per cent by December 1994.

25. There are seven development banks, each institution serving a specific role. The three major banks are Bancomext, which finances foreign trade activities, Banobras, focusing on state

and municipal project financing and Nafinsa, providing credit to small and medium-sized enterprises.

26. The System of National Accounts (SNA) would normally take into account in the general government accounts only the implicit (through guarantees or reduced dividends) or explicit subsidy component of development bank lending.

27. The figures refer to the change in total development bank credit outstanding, as reported in the Bank of Mexico monetary statistics. This differs somewhat from the definition of financial intermediation in the public accounts data. According to provisional results under the public accounts definition, financial intermediation by development banks amounted to 2.9 per cent of GDP in 1993 and 3.6 per cent in 1994.

28. The Pacts for Stability and Growth (*Pactos*) were negotiated at various intervals from December 1987 to July 1990; subsequently they were renewed yearly. For further details on the role of social concertation in the disinflation process, see OECD (1992), *Economic Survey of Mexico*.

29. See for example Dornbusch and Werner (1994).

30. Adjusting for exchange-rate valuation effects reduces these growth rates, since these aggregates are partly denominated in US dollars. On this basis, growth of broad monetary aggregates decelerated in 1994 compared with 1993.

31. Calculated from the change in the peso value of development banks' total credit outstanding, as reported by the Banco de Mexico.

32. For discussion of Mexico's financial deregulation, see Part IV.

33. In its May 1994 Report on Monetary Policy, the Bank of Mexico noted the risk of a negative impact on financial intermediaries if interest rates were raised more sharply in response to exchange-rate pressures. This policy consideration was spelled out more fully in the January 1995 Report explaining the rationale for the choice of strategy in 1994.

34. The perceived problem of conversion risk arises from the fact that Tesobonos are indexed to the dollar/peso exchange rate but payable in pesos. Market participants felt there was a risk that redemptions in pesos would not be readily exchangeable for dollars at the exchange rate applied in calculation of the redemption values (the ''fixing rate''), either due to volatility or illiquidity in the foreign exchange market, or to a perceived risk of exchange controls being introduced.

35. The peso exchange rate had already dropped to close to 5 NP/$ at the start of 1995. The government assumed that it would strengthen subsequently. The exchange rate of 4.50 NP/$ represents a depreciation of 22 per cent from the 3.50 NP/$ assumption on which the original budget projections of November 1994 had been based.

36. Current spending was to be reduced by 0.8 per cent of GDP, and capital expenditure by 0.4 per cent.

37. Training for the unemployed and displaced workers is traditionally provided through PROBECAT, the main instrument of active labour market policies (consisting of a small stipend and courses lasting from three to six months). In 1994, 200 000 scholarships were granted through PROBECAT, compared with 52 000 on average per year in 1984-89.

38. Details on PROCAMPO are presented in Part IV.

39. This switch will eventually be reflected in a change in the relative share of the internal and external components of total debt.

40. In a situation of high and unstable inflation, the use of an inflation-adjusted reference unit to denominate financial instruments offers advantages to both borrowers and investors: the risk premium being reduced, the real interest rate can be lower, and the maturity longer, than would otherwise be the case. UDIs are also being used as part of the loan restructuring programme for commercial banks (see section below). In Chile, indexed financial instruments, introduced in the 1960s and stepped up after the 1981-82 crisis, have been instrumental in lengthening the maturity of financial instruments.

41. For technical discussion of this concept and its role in monetary policy, see Part III.

42. For further discussion of the banks' prudential supervisory system, see Part IV.

43. There is no significant direct effect of depreciation on the Mexican banks' balance sheets. The banks were prevented from having direct net foreign exchange exposures in excess of 15 per cent of their capital and, accordingly, their foreign currency liabilities have been approximately matched by foreign-currency-denominated assets. In the aggregate, banks held a positive net position in foreign currencies, so the direct effect of depreciation on their net position was a small profit.

44. Some commercial banks violated a disposition of the central bank concerning limits on foreign currency loans to borrowers without adequate hedge, and will face sanctions by the financial authorities in these cases.

45. In May 1995, Banco Bilbao Vizcaya, the Spanish institution, bought 70 per cent of Mercantil Probursa, the first Mexican bank to be owned by foreign investors.

46. Details of these international experiences are discussed in "Implications of Financial Stress for Economic Recovery", OECD *Economic Outlook* No. 54, December 1993, and Edey and Hviding (1995).

47. Conditions are defined in terms of achieving policy targets, such as central bank domestic credit growth and the Federal government budget rather than performance variables such as real GDP growth, inflation and the current account balance, so that disbursements have not been affected by the March revisions to official projections. In addition, Mexico has committed itself to provide timely reports on financial and economic conditions.

48. The US$7.75 billion standby loan was to be supplemented by a US$10 billion contribution from central banks of non-G10 countries. As these have not been made available, the entire US$17.8 billion would be drawn from the IMF's own resources, if necessary.

49. US funds were authorised for use in redeeming Tesobonos and other short-term financial instruments, and strengthening foreign exchange reserves only, and were not available for refinancing of banks' external debt.

50. According to central bank estimates based on regressions over the period 1989-94, a 10 per cent depreciation adds about 5 percentage points to CPI inflation in one year. The estimated impact of the VAT rate increase is around 2 percentage points.

51. The open unemployment rate is based on the National Survey of Urban Unemployment, which covers a labour force of only about 12 million people, compared with 25 million according to the National Employment Survey, carried out every two years. There are other reasons, besides the difference in coverage, why not all job losses are reflected as increases in the open unemployment rate. First, as in most other OECD countries, discouraged workers are likely to drop out of the labour force. Second, because there is no unemployment insurance, many people cannot afford to stay unemployed even for a short period, and will find a job in the informal sector – thus being recorded as employed.

52. In 1994, general government net lending in OECD countries (excluding Iceland, Luxembourg, New Zealand, Mexico, Turkey and Switzerland) was on average –3.9 per cent of GDP and ranged from –0.2 per cent of GDP for Norway to –12.5 per cent of GDP for Greece. Net financial liabilities (net debt) amounted to 41.5 per cent of GDP on average, ranging from a net asset position of 14.3 per cent of GDP for Norway, through to a net liabilities position of 127.8 per cent of GDP for Belgium.

53. See for example OECD (1994).

54. Or maintaining balance despite weaker revenue than expected.

55. It would also be helpful to develop full National Accounts for the general government sector, by including states and municipalities and excluding public enterprises. This would allow better integration of general government analysis within the overall macroeconomic framework.

56. These affect the estimation of the production potential of the economy and also, in the tax area, the estimation of tax elasticities. An alternative and informative approach, provided in the Australian and Canadian budgets, shows a breakdown of the budget projections into changes due to policy changes and changes in economic/technical parameters. The Congressional Budget Office of the United States publishes a similar breakdown.

57. In the United States, both the Administration and the Congress provide budget estimates until 2000, in Canada the most recent budget includes fiscal projections until 1996/97 fiscal year. In Australia, the most recent budget includes projections until the 1998/99 fiscal year. In New Zealand, the government is required by law to publish fiscal projections for the coming 10 years. For EU countries, the Maastricht criteria – a 3 per cent deficit to be reached before moving to monetary union and a cap on public debt of 60 per cent of GDP – provide a medium-term objective. In this context, virtually all EU countries have prepared convergence plans, of which several elements have been published.

58. Most governments build in 3 to 5 years of forward estimates in their budget planning process, although these are not always published (see OECD *Economic Outlook* No. 55, June 1994).

59. See OECD (1995), *Economic Survey of Norway*.

60. For example, under rural development, targets include carrying out 5 100 investigations into agricultural and forestry development as well as controlling and maintaining surveillance on 27 million hectares of forest, and under tourism, generating US$4,900 million of foreign exchange and attracting 7.7 million visitors. See *Presupuesto de Egresos de la Federación para el Ejercicio Fiscal 1995*, Volume 1, December 1994.

61. For details of the tax reforms over the 1987-92 period, see OECD (1992), *Economic Survey of Mexico*, pp. 124-9.

62. See Bröker (1993).

63. These include income tax, value-added tax, energy taxes and excise taxes. States may impose payroll taxes (in some states), taxes on legal instruments, and taxes on motor vehicles that are older than 10 years. Municipalities can charge for public services and tax property.

64. In the United States, for example, most states operate under some type of self-imposed "balanced budget" constraint, and the states overall have generally maintained small surpluses. In Canada, in contrast, the provincial governments' budget position on a public

accounts basis, went from near balance in 1989/90 to a deficit in excess of 3½ per cent of GDP in 1992/3. Measures have been taken with the objective of redressing the situation.

65. See OECD (1994), *Economic Survey of the United States*, for a discussion of issues concerning very decentralised arrangements for education.

66. The stock of net domestic credit to which the ceiling applies is defined as the monetary base *minus* the peso value of international reserves (excluding borrowed reserves obtained under the international liquidity support programme and not yet applied to debt amortisation).

67. For a discussion of currency boards, see Schwartz (1993) and Walters and Hanke (1992).

68. The policies of Israel and Chile are analysed in Helpman *et al.* (1994).

69. The two airlines (Aeromexico and Mexicana) were sold in 1989, the telephone company (Telmex) in 1990, the steel company (Sidermex) in 1991 and the 19 commercial banks, which had been taken over in 1982, were privatised in 1990-92 (see below). Most divestiture deals have been private placements, with the exception of the Telmex sell-off. The phone company's controlling stake was sold through an auction. A global initial public offering (IPO) was later followed by successive placements for the remaining public participation. The shares are now being traded both in Mexico and on the New York Stock Exchange. Generally, purchasers have been Mexican business groups associated with foreign investors. Telmex, for instance, is now controlled by Grupo Carso with France Telecom and SBC Communications (formerly Southwestern Bell).

70. However, while the petrochemical industry is in theory a competitive sector, its main input, *i.e.* natural gas supplies, remains a public sector monopoly.

71. In particular, the Mexican constitution includes oil extraction and basic petrochemicals among the ''strategic'' sectors reserved exclusively for State participation, while limiting foreign investment in secondary petrochemicals to a 40 per cent equity share.

72. See OECD (1994), *Economic Survey of Italy*, p. 95.

73. On the other hand, private operators compete with Telcel (a Telmex subsidiary) in the cellular telephone market. Due to technological limitations that existed when the relevant regulations were issued, two bands were created in each of the nine regions into which the country was divided, with Telcel operating in each of them and effectively being the only national carrier. In 1994, the Federal Competition Commission (see below) authorised Grupo Iusacell (a joint-venture in which Bell Atlantic holds a 42 per cent stake), concessionaire of the Mexico City area, to take over companies serving four other regions. The Commission authorised the mergers on the grounds that they would tend to create a national network able to provide a real alternative to Telcel and therefore to introduce more competition.

74. Several consortia have already been established to compete with Telmex, among which the largest associate respectively AT&T and Grupo Alfa, MCI and Banamex and GTE and Bancomer.

75. A more determined effort to privatise CFE was partially held over on account of the bearish attitude of international investors after the December 1994 devaluation. Mexican authorities decided against selling off assets, and announced instead that they will sell securities backed by the plants' future revenues.

76. See World Bank (1994), Box 5.6, p. 99.

77. Private investors have concentrated their holdings in the most profitable airports and infrastructure, while the public sector remains responsible for most physical investment.

78. Wharfage fees are charged every time ships unload cargo in port and are generally related to the weight of the shipment that moves over the docks. The government will limit its role to monitoring that maximum rates do not exceed 4 per cent of the final value of the product shipped.

79. In particular, since 1993 the Commission has assessed the participation of 34 potential buyers in privatisation auctions involving seven companies.

80. The early stages of the deregulation process were reviewed in detail in OECD (1992), *Economic Survey of Mexico*, pp. 169-79.

81. Balance-sheet problems generated by this growth, and policy responses, are discussed in Parts I and II.

82. See Edey and Hviding (1995).

83. The National Banking Commission (CNB) was merged in May 1995 with the supervisory agency responsible for the securities industry, to form the National Banking and Securities Commission (CNBV).

84. The latter was partly prompted by a major problem arising from intra-group lending involving Cremi and Union Banks which were both part of the same business group.

85. The specific measures were, first, an increase in minimum loan-loss reserves to the greater part of 4 per cent of the loan portfolio or 60 per cent of past-due loans. Most banks at the time fell short of these standards and on average required increased reserves of around 1 per cent of loans to comply. Second, improved disclosure requirements were announced with respect to banks' reports to the CNBV, including reporting of market valuations of security portfolios and reporting of past-due loans under US GAAP standards.

86. While 3.5 million farmers, about half of the total, own plots smaller than 2 hectares, there are approximately 1.2 million farmers whose property have an average size of 68 hectares. For more details on Mexican agriculture, see OECD (1992), *Economic Survey of Mexico*, pp. 157-69.

87. Created in 1917 in the aftermath of the Revolution, *ejidos* and communal lands comprised by the late 1980s roughly a half of total land, often in remote areas.

88. Maximum property size for basic crops is limited to 100 hectares of irrigated land, or its "equivalent" in less productive rain-fed lands or pastures. No single *ejidario* can acquire more than 5 per cent of the land in any *ejido* community, and corporate entities are limited to two plots of 500 hectares of irrigated land per company.

89. This figure is based on a methodology that is different from the standard OECD one. Estimates are currently being prepared by the OECD Directorate for Food, Agriculture and Fisheries for its review of agricultural policies in Mexico.

90. As regards Mexico and the United States, agricultural non-tariff barriers were converted to either tariff-rate quotas (TRQs) or to ordinary tariffs. While existing duties on a broad range of products were eliminated as early as January 1994, adjustment periods of up to 15 years are in place for the phasing out of tariffs on sensitive produce, such as maize and dry beans for Mexico and orange juice, winter fruits and vegetables and sugar for the United States.

91. This is especially true for those that depend on maize, whose competitiveness is very low *vis-à-vis* NAFTA competitors (average yields in the United States are four times higher than in Mexico).

92. For many small maize producers, the production subsidies received were lower than the consumption tax (imposed by high domestic prices) that they suffered; subsistence farmers

(who produce for self consumption) did not benefit, nor did landless workers, and neither had access to consumption subsidies, available through shops essentially located in urban areas.

93. The successful experience of Grameen Bank in Bangladesh constitutes a working model that could be used as an example in the Mexican context. The Bank provides credit and organisational input to the poor, replacing the requirement of material collateral by group responsibility where individual access to credit is determined by group repayment behaviour. This approach has delivered impressive results in terms of loan recovery rate (consistently over 90 per cent).

94. General minimum wages are fixed by a tripartite agreement between labour unions, business representatives and the government. There are three levels for the minimum wage according to geographic area. In recent years, an income equivalent to two minimum wages has been the official threshhold set for operational purpose in the fight against poverty.

95. According to official estimates, the education backlog that confronts the authorities was made up (in 1990) of some 6 million adult people (over 15 years of age) who were illiterate; 11 million adults having started but not completed elementary school; and 1.7 million youngsters (aged between 10 and 14) who were not enrolled in school.

96. Mexico also shows a skewed structure of educational qualifications: the number of persons with intermediate/technical qualifications is fairly limited in relation to needs while there is a large pool of people with tertiary-level qualifications in traditional academic and professional fields. The growing employment problems of those with higher education, coupled with widespread concerns in the Mexican business community for the lack of qualified technicians, give some indication of mismatch in the labour market.

97. The informal sector encompasses micro-enterprises – *i.e.* firms employing five people or less – and the self-employed with little or no education above elementary schooling (excluding professionals).

98. See World Bank (1995).

99. Although it may be effective to develop some type of apprenticeship, it would be illusory to suppose that the mechanism could play the same key role as in countries where it is – and has been for a long time – an established institution. Steedman (1993) observes that the apprenticeship system works in Germany because young people who enter it have achieved a good level of school attainment, teaching is done by ''trained'' trainers, and employers and trade unions are jointly committed to make the system work.

100. PROBECAT is a labour retraining programme for unemployed and displaced workers introduced in 1984 to reduce the social impact of adjustment and facilitate the redeployment of labour. Its evaluation has shown that, while effective in improving the participants' job prospects, PROBECAT was not a substitute for prior work experience: it is, therefore, suggested that new entrants into the labour force should be supported through other policy instruments (Revenga *et al.*, 1994).

101. See IMSS (1995), p. 1. In the new Chilean private system, workers pay a mandatory contribution equivalent to 13 per cent of the wage bill, to the administrator of a pension fund of their choosing. Retirees in the former pay-as-you-go public system receive their pension out of the general government budget, to the tune of 3 per cent of GDP annually. The pension reform is widely regarded as one of the key factors underlying the rise of Chile's domestic saving ratio and contributing to the development of financial markets. It

has been used as a blue-print for similar reforms both in Central Europe and in other Latin American countries (such as Argentina and Peru).

102. Only the basic health basket, covering a minimum of health services, would be subsidised. People would be allowed to choose a family doctor and everyone should be accepted into any plan, although some risk adjustment (of premia) could be considered.

103. The extremely poor are those who cannot acquire a basket of basic goods providing a minimum acceptable level of nutrition and other necessities of everyday life. Econometric evidence showing that the elasticity of formal employment to GDP growth is lower than unity highlights the limited scope of simple trickle-down effects in improving living conditions for the lot of the Mexican poor (Davila *et al.*, 1994). In a study on income distribution in Chile, Marcel and Solimano (1993) show that growth had a significant impact only when the economy approached full capacity, a situation from which Mexico seems to be far away.

104. Such links have been highlighted by the literature on the East Asian "miracle" and the "endogenous growth" theory. It has been maintained that the accumulation of human capital that contributed to rising real incomes in East Asian newly-industrialised economies was brought about by their structure of income and wealth distribution, which set them apart from other developing countries. Rapid growth in East Asian countries was helped by unusually low income inequality in the 1960s, which led to the adoption of policies aimed at accumulating human capital. At the same time, narrow income distribution contributed to avoiding populist policies which usually bring about uncertainty and therefore discourage investment activity. The export-oriented and labour-demanding pattern of growth later came as a support element, further reinforcing the equitable structure of income distribution in countries such as Korea and Taiwan. On the other hand, in Latin America and in many other industrialising economies such as Turkey, uneven income distribution has been accompanied by insufficient social spending on primary health care and alphabetisation, pricing policies that have been to the detriment of rural sectors, and industrial strategies favouring capital- rather than labour-intensive technologies. See Alesina and Perotti (1994), Aturupane *et al.* (1994), Birsdall and Sabot (1995), and Persson and Tabellini (1994).

105. Mexican social policies were already subjected to a detailed review in OECD (1992), *Economic Survey of Mexico*, pp. 98-117.

106. Extreme poverty is defined as a total monetary income which is not enough to supply a family with its feeding needs. Over the 1989-93 period, the number of the extremely poor diminished by 1.3 million (from 14.9 to 13.6 million), while total population rose by 5 million (to 84 million); the reduction in the number of extremely poor occurred essentially in urban areas, while in rural areas the number of extremely poor people was unchanged (see INEGI-ECLAC, 1993).

107. The biggest drawback of social indicators is that they measure national averages, and are, therefore, sensitive to differences in distribution.

108. It should be noted, however, that the rate of population growth in Mexico City slowed considerably after the devastating 1985 earthquake. More generally, the population share of the four metropolitan areas (Mexico City, Guadalajara, Monterrey and Puebla) decreased from 51.3 per cent in 1980 to 45 per cent in 1990, the last census year.

109. During the 1980s, despite cuts in government programmes in pursuit of fiscal consolidation, progress in the access to and achievements of education continued, although at a slower pace than previously.

110. See Graham (1994). However, Solidarity differs from most other social investment funds in Latin America because it is administered as an annual budgetary appropriation programme and has never been established as an autonomous fund.

111. The Social Development Agreements (Convenios de Desarrollo Social) establish the broad framework for federal-state co-operation, within which budgetary allocations for each Solidarity programme and specific investments are agreed each year between SEDESOL and the State Planning Committee (COPLADE).

112. A similar programme, the Integral programme to correct the educational lag (PAIRE), co-ordinates actions in nine other states. The World Bank contributes 75 per cent of the total estimated cost (US$500 million), while states finance the rest.

113. In 1989-92, for example, 273 hospitals were either built or renovated, 655 rural towns were electrified and more than 123 000 km of roads went through maintenance. Of course, it is very difficult to judge whether public works done within Solidarity's framework would have been done anyway.

114. Salinas de Gortari (1994), p. 53.

115. The Tortivales programme allows participating households to receive one kilo of free *tortillas* a day from participating shops, whereas Liconsa allows milk to be purchased at one-quarter of the market price.

116. In the case of the school breakfast programme, the bias in favour of urban areas is due to easier access.

117. Graham (1994), p. 270.

118. From a political science perspective, it has been observed that the role of Solidarity in the transition from a clientelistic polity, based on patronage, to a fully-fledged democracy, well beyond the minimum threshold of competitive elections, is mixed. The result is rather "the coexistence under the same formal regime of three different *de facto* political systems: entrenched redoubts of authoritarianism, broad swaths of modernised semiclientelism, and enclaves of pluralist tolerance" (Fox, 1994, p. 183).

119. See World Bank (1993).

120. In terms of number of inhabitants per clinic, private medical services are concentrated in the capital cities of richer states. The geographical bias is not as pronounced in the case of social security, but there is still a concentration of facilities in urban areas where the insured population lives. On the other hand, the distribution of public health facilities reflects a greater concern with equity: as is the case for the other two systems, public health clinics are concentrated in the Federal District, but elsewhere in the country more health facilities tend to be located in rural areas than in capitals, and in the poorest Southern states rather than in the North.

121. Although a large share of the social security budget comes from employers' and employees' contributions, the government directly contributes about 5 per cent of the budget and covers the eventual deficit (IMSS health services actually recorded a surplus in 1989-90 and small deficits ever since).

References

Alesina, A. and R. Perotti (1994), "The Political Economy of Growth: A Critical Survey of the Recent Literature", *The World Bank Economic Review*, Vol. 8, No. 3.

Appendini, K. (1992), *De la milpa a los tortibonos. la restructuración de la política alimentaria en México*, El Colegio de México, Mexico City.

Aturupane, H., P. Glewwe, and P. Isenman (1994), "Poverty, Human Development, and Growth: An Emerging Consensus?", *American Economic Review, Papers and Proceedings*, Vol. 84, No. 2.

Bell, L. (1994), "The Impact of Minimum Wages in Mexico and Colombia", mimeo, presented to the World Bank Labor Markets Workshop, Washington, July 6-8.

Birsdall, N. and R. Sabot (1995), "Inequality as a Constraint on Growth in Latin America", in D. Turnham, C. Foy and G. Larraín (eds.), *Social Tensions, Job Creation and Economic Policy in Latin America*, OECD, Paris.

Bishop, M, J. Kay and C. Mayer (1995), "Introduction", in M. Bishop, J. Kay and C. Mayer (eds.), *The Regulatory Challenge*, Oxford University Press, Oxford.

Bröker, G. (1993), *Government Securities and Debt Management in the 1990s*, OECD, Paris.

Buira, A. (1994), "The Main Determinants of Savings in Mexico", mimeo, presented to the Conference on the role of saving in economic growth, Federal Reserve Bank of Dallas, March 18-19.

Dávila, E., S. Levy and L. F. López Calva (1994), "Empleo rural y combate a la pobreza: una propuesta de política", mimeo.

Dornbusch, R. and A. Werner (1994), "Mexico: Stabilization, Reform, and No Growth", *Brookings Papers on Economic Activity*, Vol. 1.

Edey, M. and K. Hviding (1995), "An Assessment of Financial Reform in OECD Countries", *OECD Economics Department Working Paper*, No. 154, Paris.

Fox, J. (1994), "The Difficult Transition from Clientelism to Citizenship: Lessons from Mexico", *World Politics*, Vol. 46, No. 2.

Frenk, J., R. Lozano, and M. González-Black (1994), *Economía y Salud: Propuestas para el Avance del Sistema de Salud en México*, FUNSALUD, Mexico City.

Graham, C. (1994), *Safety Nets, Politics, and the Poor*, The Brookings Institution, Washington.

135

Grosh, M. (1994), *Administering Targeted Social Programs in Latin America*, The World Bank, Washington.

Helpman, E., L. Leiderman and G. Bufman (1994), "A new breed of exchange rate bands: Chile, Israel and Mexico", *Economic Policy*, No. 19.

IMSS (1995), *Diagnostico*, Mexico City.

INEGI-ECLAC (1993), *Magnitude and evolution of poverty in Mexico, 1984-92*, Mexico City.

Levy, S. and S. van Wijnbergen (1994), "Labor Markets, Migration and Welfare: Agriculture in the North-American Free Trade Agreement", *Journal of Development Economics*, Vol. 43, No. 2.

Marcel, M. and A. Solimano (1994), "The Distribution of Income and Economic Adjustment", in B. Bosworth, R. Dornbusch and R. Labán (eds.), *The Chilean Economy*, The Brookings Institution, Washington.

Mexico (1995), *National Report for the World Summit on Social Development*, Copenhagen.

OECD (1994), *Taxation and Household Saving*, Paris.

Ozorio de Almeida, A., S. Graham and L. Alves (1994), "Poverty, Deregulation and Informal Employment in Mexico", mimeo, The World Bank, Washington.

Patrinos, H. A. (1994), "The Costs of Discrimination in Latin America", The World Bank, *ESP Discussion Paper*, No. 32, Washington.

Persson, T. and G. Tabellini (1994), "Is Inequality Harmful for Growth?", *American Economic Review*, Vol. 84, No. 3.

Revenga, A., M. Riboud and H. Tan (1994), "The Impact of Mexico's Retraining Program on Employment and Wages", *The World Bank Economic Review*, Vol. 8, No. 2.

Salinas de Gortari, C. (1994), *Sexto Informe de Gobierno*, Presidencia de la República, Dirección General de Comunicación Social, Mexico City.

Schwartz, A. (1993), "Currency Boards: Their Past, Present and Future Role", *Carnegie-Rochester Conference Series on Public Policy*, No. 39.

Steedman, H. (1993), "The Economics of Youth Training in Germany", *The Economic Journal*, Vol. 103, No. 5.

United States Department of Agriculture (1994), *Estimates of Producer Subsidy Equivalents and Consumer Subsidy Equivalents: Government Intervention in Agriculture, 1982-1992*, Washington.

Walters, A. and S. Hanke (1992), "Currency Boards", in P. Newman, M. Milgate and J. Eatwell (eds.), *The New Palgrave Dictionary of Money and Finance*, McMillan, London.

World Bank (various years), *World Development Report*, Oxford University Press, Oxford.

Annex I

Background Tables

Table A1. **Domestic marketable public debt instruments in selected OECD countries in 1990** [1]

	Short term instruments (Treasury bills) [2]	Per cent of total	Medium and long term instruments	Per cent of total
Mexico [3]	Cetes: 28, 91, 182, 364 days [4]	17.6	Ajustabonos: 3, 5 years	12.6
	Tesobonos: 91, 182, 364 days	66.3	Bondes: 1, 2, 10 years	3.5
United States	13, 26, 52 weeks	24.2	Treasury notes: 2-10 years	58.0
			Treasury bonds: 30 years	17.8
Germany	None	0.0	Treasury discount notes: 1, 2 years	0.3
			Medium term federal notes: 4 years	10.4
			5-year special federal notes	29.0
			Federal bonds: mostly 10 years	60.4
France	13, 26, 52 weeks	9.4	Treasury notes: 2, 5 years	28.5
			Fungible government bonds: 5-30 years	51.9
			Other medium to long term bonds	10.2
Italy	3, 6, 12 months	30.1	Treasury option certificates: 6 year (with 3-year early redemption)	5.7
			Treasury bonds: 3-10 years	21.7
			Treasury floating rate certificates: 7 years	37.5
			Other	5.0
United Kingdom	91 and 182 days and occasional shorter-dated bills	10.5	Bonds: less than 5 years to 40 years index-linked non-index-linked	15.8 73.7
Canada	3, 5, 12 months	49.5	Government bonds: 2-30 years	50.5
			Index-linked bonds: 30 years	
Greece	3, 6, 12 months	80.5	Floating rate government bonds: 2-5 years	7.2
			ECU-linked government bonds: 1-5 years	12.3
Turkey	3, 6, 9 months	42.5	Government bonds: 1-5 years	57.5

1. Excluding issues for cash management purposes only.
2. Up to one year.
3. At end of 1994.
4. A 2-year Cetes instrument was introduced in 1993, but forms a very small part of the outstanding stock.
Source: OECD.

Table A2. **The regulation of fixed-link telephony in selected countries**

	Mexico		United States	Japan	United Kingdom	Chile
Ownership/date of privatisation	Private/1990		Private 1934[1]	Private/1985	Private/1984	Private/1985-86
Date of regulation	1990	1995		n.a.	1984	1982
Structure of industry	Integrated	Integrated	Functionally separated	Integrated	Integrated[2]	Integrated
Structure of market						
Local calls	Monopoly	Competitive	Local monopoly	Monopoly	Duopoly[3]	Competitive
Long-distance calls	Monopoly	Competitive	Competitive	Monopoly	Duopoly[3]	Competitive
Regulatory institutions	Ministerial	Independent	Ministerial	Ministerial	Independent	Ministerial
Type of regulation						
Price						
Local calls	RPI-X[4]	RPI-X[5]	Rate of return	Rate of return	RPI-X[6]	Marginal cost
Long-distance calls	RPI-X	RPI-X[5]	None	Rate of return	RPI-X[6]	None
Quality	Yes	Yes	No	No	No[7]	Yes
Promotion of competition	No	Yes	No	No	Yes	Yes
Arbitration	Judiciary	Judiciary	Fair trade commission	Fair trade commission	Monopoly and merger commission	Judiciary
Renegotiation	Fixed-term	Discretionary[8]	Discretionary	Discretionary	Fixed-term	Fixed-term

1. Major changes were introduced with the 1982 Consent Decree that broke up the Bell system.
2. Companies are required to keep separate accounts for different operations.
3. Partial liberalisation in 1989.
4. Regulated services include installation and rental charges, measured local, domestic and international long-distance calls. X was set at zero over the 1991-96 period and at 3 over the following two years.
5. Telmex only.
6. The basket of regulated services currently includes 70 per cent of British Telecom's business. X was raised from 3 over the 1984-89 period to 7.5 over the 1993-97 period.
7. A mixture of fixed penalties and contractual liabilities was introduced in 1987.
8. Length of concession fixed by law.

Source: Adapted from Goldstein, A. and G. Nicoletti (1995), "Italian Privatisations in International Perspective", *Econpubblica Working Paper*, No. 33, Università Bocconi, Milan.

Table A3. **The main programme elements of Solidarity**
NP billion

		Type of programme [1]	1990 [2]	1991 [2]	1992 [3]	1993 [4]
1.	Health and adequate hospital	W	191.5	190.8	455.6	405.0
2.	Educational infrastructure	W	278.6	429.6	860.9	610.0
3.	Children of solidarity	W	0.0	145.0	470.4	638.7
4.	Sports facilities	I	45.6	79.9	173.6	150.0
5.	Solidarity in neighbourhood and communities [5]	W	208.0	380.3	1 117.9	675.0
6.	Drinking water and sewage	I	357.3	547.5	1 887.8	675.0
7.	Electrification	W	173.9	267.8	500.8	280.0
8.	Adequate housing	I	48.5	89.1	96.2	150.0
9.	National fund for solidarity businesses [6]	P	0.0	0.0	369.7	400.0
10.	Solidarity funds for production [7]	P	395.4	378.6	850.8	900.0
11.	Regional development programmes	RD	484.8	794.2	965.8	818.7
12.	Rural roads and motorways	RD	370.4	747.8	1 569.5	800.0
13.	Municipal solidarity funds	RD	258.4	319.7	946.7	650.0
14.	Solidarity for social service	W	63.7	130.3	169.8	170.0
15.	Women in solidarity	S	18.2	31.7	61.0	50.0
16.	Indigenous communities	S	134.5	220.3	158.4	375.0
17.	Supply and commercialisation	P	32.7	27.0	47.4	..
18.	Others	n.a.	215.9	406.2	160.0	..
Total			3 277.4	5 185.8	10 882.3	7 747.4

1. I = infrastructure; P = productive; RD = regional development; S = special; W = welfare.
2. Resources exercised.
3. Estimated close.
4. Planned budget.
5. Includes programmes co-ordinated with CONASUPO, such as Liconsa and Tortivales.
6. Includes programmes for small coffee growers, carried out in co-ordination with INI.
7. Created to assist peasants excluded from BANRURAL's coverage.
Source: Hacienda Pública Federal Account for the year stated.

Table A4. **Regions by mortality rates**

Region A	(Low infant and adult mortality rates)	Aguascalientes, Baja California Sur, Coahuila, Distrito Federal, Nayarit, Nuevo León, Sinaloa, Sonora, Tamaulipas.
Region B	(Low infant and high adult mortality rates)	Baja California Norte, Chihuahua, Colima, Jalisco, Morelos, Tabasco.
Region C	(Average infant and low adult mortality rates)	Campeche, Guanajuato, Quintana Roo, San Luis Potosí, Tlaxcala, Yucatán, Zacatecas.
Region D	(High infant and adult mortality rates and large urban-rural difference)	Durango, México, Michoacán, Querétaro, Veracruz.
Region E	(High infant and adult mortality rates)	Chiapas, Hidalgo, Guerrero, Oaxaca, Puebla.

Source: Frenk, J., R. Lozano and M. Gonzales-Black (1994), *Economía y salud*, FUNSALUD, Mexico City.

Annex II

Fiscal federalism

The appropriate allocation of responsibilities and functions to different levels of government has been an issue in a number of OECD countries in recent years. In general, changes over the last 20 years or so have resulted in responsibilities being reallocated away from the central government,[1] either downwards to lower levels of governments (state, regional, metropolitan, municipal, etc.) or upwards to a supra-national level as in the case of the European Union countries. In this annex, the main conceptual issues that would generally arise in any discussion of reforms are presented and the arrangements prevailing in Mexico and other OECD countries are briefly reviewed. It should be noted however, that historical and political considerations, which also play an important role, are not taken into account in this annex.[2]

Conceptual issues

There are relatively few public sector activities which indisputably "belong" to one level of government or another – external security and street lighting are straightforward examples of national and local public goods respectively. For many activities, the central (or federal) government may have objectives that it wishes to achieve while at the same time, each local area may have different views about the appropriate overall level and the mix of government services that it prefers. The appropriate distribution of responsibilities for these activities depends on finding a balance between central government objectives and responsiveness to local preferences.

Public policy objectives can be divided into three broad groups: macroeconomic, allocative, and distributive.[3] It is generally accepted that macroeconomic policy is most effectively set at the national level: attempts by individual states or local governments to conduct an independent fiscal policy will be ineffective because of the openness of the local economy and the use of national monetary policy. Nevertheless, it is possible for states or local governments to undermine the central government's fiscal policy stance through their borrowing activity.[4] A sound macroeconomic policy framework may thus imply some constraints on the borrowing capacity of lower levels of government in order to achieve a consistent fiscal policy stance.[5]

141

Except for national public goods, allocative policies can be assigned to local communities, who can identify the amount and type of local public goods they wish to consume, and the outcome will be efficient, as long as the local taxes are set to reflect the benefits that members of the local community receive. However, many of the services provided by government are not pure public goods and consumers could be charged for them according to their usage. For services such as water, sewage, rubbish disposal etc., local needs and costs vary widely, externalities are relatively localised and/or low and local provision and charging structures are appropriate. However, other services, such as health, education, housing etc., are often provided to some or all of the population, free or at a low charge to consumers either because some people would otherwise be unable to afford them or because they would choose to consume less than the government considers desirable (*i.e.* a merit good). In either case, such services embody a redistributive element.

Distributive policies, especially those which are embodied in the provision or funding of merit goods, are less easy to assign unambiguously to a particular level of government. Attempts by one state or local authority to operate a significantly different distributive policy than others may result in migration of the poor towards the more generous area and the rich away from it,[6] leading to a lower degree of overall redistribution than would be achieved through centralised policies.[7] But there may be greater concern for the poor of a local community than for the poor elsewhere, leading local communities to go further towards meeting the needs of those within their midst than they would be willing to do under a centralised policy.[8] It could also be argued that accountability is enhanced and the scope for abuse is reduced because the local community has both a greater incentive and a greater capacity to monitor policies and programmes closely. A normative issue in redistributive policy also arises: whether the objective is to redistribute income between richer and poorer individuals or between richer and poorer communities.[9] In any case, central government may wish to maintain some influence over policy settings even where much of the responsibility for provision is devolved to lower levels of government, meaning that some sharing of responsibility and coordination of policy will generally evolve for those activities involving a degree of redistribution.

Funding arrangements

Funding arrangements between different levels of government can take a number of forms depending on the degree and nature of control exercised by the central government (see Figure A1). One option is to provide funding for specific programmes under tightly defined conditions (which nevertheless may be tailored to the local circumstances of each area). In this case, the lower level of government has little decision making power and is simply acting as the agent of the central government in the administration of the programme.[10] Tight controls on how funds are spent may also limit innovation by state/local governments: innovation and experimentation at the local level has been one of the ways in which successful programmes and policies tried first in one locality have progressively supplanted less successful ones in other areas.

TAXONOMY OF FUNDING OPTIONS FOR LOWER LEVELS OF GOVERNNMENT

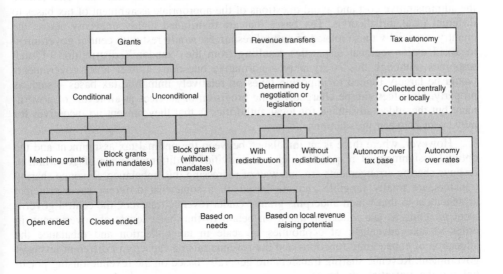

Another option is "matching" grants for the provision of specific services which provide an incentive structure and a degree of flexibility that encourages lower levels of governments to provide the appropriate services at least cost (because local governments must allocate part of their resources as well). Open-ended matching grants encourage local governments to internalise spatial externalities and ensure that the appropriate level of spending needed to internalise the externality does take place. Closed-ended matching grants (*i.e.* grants with a ceiling on the central government funding contribution) encourage the provision of minimum levels (leaving it open to the local government to provide additional services if it wishes).

A still more flexible form would be for the central government to provide sectoral block grants[11] based on broad criteria such as, for education, the number of children covered by a local authority, or a general block grant based, for example, on population characteristics. If the central government wishes to maintain some control over the way the money is spent, it may mandate minimum standards for different activities, but the grants themselves would be fungible, providing the local government with an incentive to find the least costly way of achieving the required standards and major scope for adapting policies to local needs.[12] Alternatively, the central government may pass over to local governments all control over policy settings, in which case the central government's role is simply to make grants that redistribute income between states.

The standard conceptual assignment of tax bases to different levels of government is the following.[13] Tax bases that are relatively mobile (such as income taxes or consumption taxes) would remain with central government or at least be determined centrally because of the incentives for internal migration that they would otherwise generate.[14] For income and value added taxes, centralised collection and nation-wide rates also reduce the administrative cost and avoid questions of the appropriate assignment of tax bases to different local jurisdictions. Tax bases that are distributed highly unevenly across the country, especially those related to natural resources, would rest with central government to avoid major regional disparities resulting from the "random" distribution of such resources (although this is arguably a normative question). Lower level governments would be largely limited to imposing taxes on relatively immobile tax bases – such as property. User fees can be charged for the provision of services at all levels of government but the added advantage for local authorities is that they present no incentives for movement between jurisdictions.

However, where there is an imbalance between the optimal tax assignment and the optimal assignment of responsibilities and activities to different levels of government, revenue sharing arrangements are one way of redressing this imbalance. Revenue sharing transfers are totally fungible and are based on a somewhat different agent-principal arrangement to that which underpins grants. Under revenue transfers, the central government is acting as tax collection agent on behalf of the lower levels of government, in order to take advantage of economies of scale in tax collection and rebalance the allocation of expenditure functions and the revenue raising capacity of different levels of government. Revenue sharing transfers are generally based on the revenue raising potential (or the potential tax base) of each area but may also embody some degree of redistribution based on the spending "needs" of the area. The amount of redistribution is dependent on the trade-off between richer states' willingness to pay higher taxes and their desire to discourage mobility towards them but, as noted above, the rationale for redistribution between states is a normative one.

An alternative to this approach is to grant greater fiscal autonomy to lower levels of government. This could be achieved by allowing lower levels greater freedom to impose taxes – including control over both the tax base and tax rates. This may be a matter of giving local governments more flexibility and control over their existing taxes, or reassigning some of the existing central government tax bases to lower levels, or allowing lower levels to introduce whatever taxes they wished. A major advantage of providing greater autonomy in these ways is greater fiscal transparency resulting in more direct electoral accountability. But, given the constraints that mobility imposes on tax bases available to local authorities and the economies of scale in collection, the scope for greater direct fiscal autonomy may be limited. Another option, although less transparent, is to add a non-progressive surcharge to income tax collected by the central administration, with the surcharge rate chosen by each local authority. This provides a degree of flexibility to each locality and could provide a significant source of revenue.[15]

Sub-national levels of government in OECD countries[16]

A diverse range of responsibilities and funding arrangements prevail in OECD countries, as summarised in Tables A5 and A6 but some clear patterns emerge. Responsi-

Table A5. **Activities and responsibilities of sub-national levels of government in OECD countries**[1]

	Activities and responsibilities	Employment[2]
Mexico	Management of schools (apart from teachers' pay), in health (some states only) and poverty alleviation programmes.	40
United States	*State:* Responsibility for education, public welfare, highways, hospitals and housing services, justice and police, natural resources, housing and community developments.	25
	Local: Local governments carry out their activities under delegation from the states and responsibilities vary considerably from state to state, but may include any of the states' functions listed above.	59
Japan	Primary functions include maintenance and management of facilities for health, welfare and education, police and fire fighting. Also carry out a range of functions on behalf of the central government with varying degrees of discretion.	73
Germany	*Länder:* A major part of police system, administration of justice, cultural affairs, education, some health services delivery. Länder are also responsible for implementation of around $3/4$ of all federal law.	54
France	Administrative and financial management of schools (but teachers' salaries are paid by central government), economic infrastructure, employment, development,	32
Italy	Regions are responsible for agriculture, handicrafts, small and medium sized businesses, health care, manpower training, regional public transport networks, public housing, environmental protection. Local authorities are responsible for social aid, some aspects of health care, kindergarten and primary education, culture.	28
United Kingdom	Schooling (under local education authorities), welfare services including residential and domiciliary care, environmental health, housing, planning, police, fire services.	53
Canada	*Provinces:* Each province is sovereign, but powers reserved to the federal government have led to a high degree of inter-dependence and close co-operation between the federal government and states. Main responsibility for health, public education, income security and social services programmes.	42
	Municipalities: Civil defence, transport, hygiene, planning, recreation and community services.	28
Australia	*State:* Hospital services, education (except tertiary), police and legal services.	72
	Local: Planning, community services and recreational facilities, public health and sanitary services.	10
Austria	*Länder:* Primary education, housing, health, welfare, plus the execution of most federal administrative tasks.	40
	Local: Primary schools, some kindergartens and hospitals, social and cultural activities and some tasks carried out on behalf of the Länder and the Federal government.	22

Activities and responsibilities of sub-national levels of government in OECD countries [1] *(cont'd)*

	Activities and responsibilities	Employment [2]
Belgium	Regions are responsible for land use planning, environment and waste management, public works and transport, regional economic development, natural and energy resources, promotion of employment and redeployment and supervision of local authorities. Communities (defined by language) are responsible for language and culture, education, health and direct assistance to individuals and audio-visual media. Provinces and municipalities are responsible for security and civil protection and special assignments from regions and communities such as schooling.	78
Finland	Basic education, social services, physical planning and a range of other services.	77
The Netherlands	Regions are responsible for physical planning, transport and public works, environment, recreation and supervision of municipalities (and polder boards). Municipalities have full responsibility for traffic, recreation and culture, joint responsibility for physical planning, housing, police, fire fighting, civil registration, public education and social aid.	26
Norway	Counties are responsible for hospital and other specialised health services, secondary educational and vocational training, construction and maintenance of main roads, coordination of local public transport and regional planning. Municipalities are responsible for primary education, nursery schools, domiciliary services for elderly and disabled, income support for those in need, primary health care, recreational facilities, physical planning and urban renewal.	74
Portugal	Recreation and cultural facilities, primary schools (apart from teachers' pay).	17
Spain	Cultural activities, housing, environmental protection, public works, education, health and social welfare.	47
Sweden	Counties are responsible for health and medical care, certain types of education and vocational training. Municipalities are responsible for basic education, housing, child and old-age care and cultural and leisure activities.	73
Switzerland	Law and order, health and sanitation, public works, taxation, land use, planning, cultural affairs, education, etc. Also oversee execution of most federal laws (under supervision by the federal government).	75
Turkey	Urban infrastructure, organisation and control of commercial activities, preventive and curative health measures, social security and assistance, police, recreational and cultural activities.	14

1. Standard public services such as water, sewage, rubbish disposal and local road maintenance have not been listed, although they are almost universally provided by local government.
2. Employment by sub-national levels of government as a percentage of employment by all levels of government (excluding public enterprises).
The four smallest OECD countries are not included in this analysis.
Source: OECD.

Table A6. **Revenues of sub-national levels of government in OECD countries**

	Nature of grants and transfers received	Grant income [2]	Taxes on: [1]				
			Income [3]	Property	Consumption	Other [4]	Total
Mexico	*States:* receive revenue transfers and some specific grants.	2.4	0	0	0	0	0.1
	Municipalities: receive grants via the states.	0.5	0	0	0	0	..
United States	*State:* Mixture of specific grant and block grants. By the mid-1980s block grants had fallen to less than 5 per cent of total grants.	2.3	2.2	0.2	1.8	1.4	5.6
	Local: Federal and state grants.	3.4	0.2	2.9	0.4	0.4	3.9
Japan	Grants for specific purposes, account for around 25 per cent of local revenues.	..	4.5	2.0	0	1.0	7.5
Germany	*Länder:* Some redistribution transfers between Länders take place. Also some grants are made by federal government for capital projects.	3.3	4.9	0.5	2.2	0.6	8.2
	Municipalities and Counties: Local social services, recreational and cultural facilities, hospitals and kindergartens.	3.2	2.5	0.5	0	0	3.0
France	Mostly specific grants.	3.4	1.3	0.6	0	2.2	4.1
Italy	Provinces depend almost entirely on grants from central government. Local authorities receive transfers from general and regional government.	10.0	0.5	0	0	0.7	1.2
United Kingdom	Specific grants.	8.7	0	0	0	1.3	1.3
Canada	*Provinces:* Revenue sharing arrangements based on need and fiscal capacity. Specific grants (*e.g.* cover to grants block and education) in health and social services.	3.9	5.9	0.8	2.7	2.5	11.9
	Municipalities: Grants from provinces.	3.6	0	3.3	0	0.5	3.8

Table A6. **Revenues of sub-national levels of government in OECD countries** *(cont'd)*

| | Nature of grants and transfers received | Grant income [2] | Taxes on: [1] | | | | |
			Income [3]	Property	Con-sumption	Other [4]	Total
Australia	*State:* For current expenditures, general revenue sharing is agreed by the Conference of Premiers each year. For capital, general purpose and special purpose grants are made.	7.3	0	1.7	0	3.8 [5]	5.5
	Local: Block grants paid via the states and specific grants (*e.g.* for children's services).	0.5	0	1.1	0	0	1.1
Austria	*Länder:* Finance Equalization Law, negotiated every five years governs the apportionment of joint taxes. Also specific grants for housing subsidies, teachers' salaries, etc.	3.5	2.3	0	1.6	0.7	4.6
	Local: Transfers from federal government and Länder.	1.5	2.0	0.5	1.0	1.4	4.9
Belgium	Grants and revenue sharing transfers: (regions sharing mainly income tax, communities sharing mainly VAT, and provinces and municipalities sharing mainly property tax).	..	1.7	0	0	0.5	2.2
Denmark	Parts of the central government tax-take is allocated to local authorities through block grants, distributed according to "objective criteria" such as demography and the local tax base. Furthermore, tax equalisation transfers between local authorities take place.	..	14.3	1.0	0	0	15.3
Finland	In 1985, 99 per cent of all grants were specific, but these are gradually being replaced by block grants.	7.5	9.6	0.1	0	0	9.7
Greece	As responsibilities are transferred to regions, funding is transferred with them. Local authorities receive per capita general grants and specific grants from particular central government ministries.	..	0	0	0	0.4	0.4

	Nature of grants and transfers received	Grant income [2]	Taxes on: [1]				
			Income [3]	Property	Con-sumption	Other [4]	Total
The Netherlands	Block grant and specific grants (especially for construction and management of roads).	12.0	0	0.7	0	0.3	1.0
Norway	Counties receive four sectoral block grants for secondary schools, transport, health and general income support. These grants are fully fungible between sectors. Some specific grants. Municipalities also receive sectoral grants to cover their responsibilities.	8.0	8.4	0.9	0	0.4	9.7
Portugal	Grants from central government.	2.5	0.5	0.7	0.4	0.4	2.0
Spain	Different degrees of revenue autonomy in different regions. Revenue sharing transfers apply for most regions and are based on a percentage of incomes with inter-regional transfers	8.2	0.7	1.6	0.6	1.3	4.2
Sweden	Instead of revenue sharing transfers, Sweden has a method of allocating equalising block grants according to a guaranteed share of the tax base. Specific grants from central government are also made, but these are taken into account when calculating the block grant.	4.2	17.0	0	0	0.1	17.1
Switzerland	Some transfers to support weaker cantons and communes.	..	9.6	1.6	0	0.5	11.7
Turkey	Revenue sharing transfers.	..	0.9	0.1	0.6	0.3	1.9

1. Tax classifications and the basis for attribution to different levels of government are provided in OECD (1994*b*).
2. Including revenue transfers, as a per cent of GDP for the most recent year available (in most cases, 1991 or 1992).
3. Including profits.
4. Includes specific taxes on goods and services, taxes on use, etc., payroll taxes and other.
5. Includes 1.7 per cent of GDP collected as payroll tax.
The four smallest OECD countries are not included in this analysis.
Source: OECD.

bility for the provision of many merit goods such as health and education are often devolved to lower levels rather than remaining with central government. Responsibilities in some sectors are shared between levels of government. Health and education sectors are often also split between different levels of government, for example primary schools may be a municipal responsibility while secondary schools are the responsibility of a regional level, and hospitals and home care services may be similarly split. A number of central governments also use lower levels extensively to carry out functions on their behalf. In more than half of the OECD countries considered, state and local governments play a major role in delivering general government services (whether these are fully under their control or provided on behalf of central government) with 70 per cent or more of total public sector employment[17] occurring at state and local levels. Population size is not a determining factor here as France and Italy still have relatively centralised administrations, despite decentralisation implemented during the 1980s, and Greece, Portugal and Turkey have highly centralised systems.

Many countries have a mix of specific grants and general block grants or revenue sharing transfers. The mix of grants has changed over time in a number of countries, but no clear pattern has emerged. For example, Norway moved in 1986 from specific grants to block grants, but found some resistance to relinquishing some categorical grants[18] and more recently, some new specific grants have been introduced. During the 1980s, the United States moved in the opposite direction with block grants gradually falling to a very low proportion of overall grants made[19] but there is currently discussion about the merits of moving towards greater use of block grants for Medicaid. This underlines the fact that the nature and extent of decentralisation varies from sector to sector and over time.[20]

Taxes levied by lower levels of government also vary considerably. Local tax revenues naturally tend to be relatively low in those countries with relatively centralised spending arrangements. Local tax revenues are also low relative to state and local government responsibilities in Australia, the Netherlands, Italy, Spain and the United Kingdom. Countries that do collect a significant amount of tax at the local level all rely to some extent on income tax and local governments in Denmark, Finland and Sweden rely virtually entirely on income tax revenue. However, tax rates vary relatively little, if at all, between jurisdictions, and are generally collected by central government on behalf of lower levels.

Mexico[21]

Mexico is a federation of 31 states (plus the Federal District of Mexico City) and 2 377 municipalities. Constitutionally, states and municipalities have a significant degree of autonomy, but in practice, most spending activities and revenue-raising have been concentrated at the federal level. On the expenditure side, there has often not been a clear division of functions between levels of government; some activities are state or municipal responsibilities in some parts of the country and federal responsibilities in others. Some responsibilities have been shared, most notably through the Solidarity programme for social development (described in Part V), under which part of the cost is financed by the federal government and part by the states (*i.e.* matching grants). A similar arrangement applies with the municipalities except that the municipalities' contribution is more often provided in the form of labour and materials, rather than in direct funding. However, the allocation of resources under these programmes is discretionary and there are no clear rules guiding the allocation.

Some decentralisation has also taken place in education and health. Starting in 1992, the federal government transferred the administration and operation of its 163 000 primary and secondary schools to the states, except for the schools in the Federal District. However, the federal government retains control over plans and programs of study, compulsory and optional subjects, choice of text books, the length of the school year, and the general conditions for the recruitment and promotion of teachers. In practice, the federal government also negotiates teachers' pay and conditions. Less decentralisation has taken place in the health sector[22] and only 13 states have opted for decentralised agreements, although decentralisation of health started in 1983. Where decentralisation has taken place, states share the costs of operating public health clinics according to agreements between the state and the federal government, although the state's contribution varies significantly. The states can either set up a state department of health providing services directly, or a semi-autonomous administrative agency or both. Some states have decentralised health care further to the municipal level.

On the revenue side, the Constitution sets out some boundaries on taxes that can be levied by different levels of government. Only the federal government may impose taxes on foreign trade, natural resources, credit institutions, and a range of special taxes on production of particular goods and services. The states do not have any tax bases reserved to them, but are prohibited from imposing taxes on the transit of persons or goods and services. Only municipalities can impose property taxes. In practice, while income and consumption taxes could be imposed by any level, they are governed by accords between the federal government and the states, under the System of Fiscal Co-ordination. This system, instituted in 1980, provides for revenue sharing transfers based on each state's capacity to raise revenue and its population. The federal government also makes transfers to the municipalities, but these are discretionary rather than governed by clearly defined formulae. Both states and municipalities are heavily reliant on the transfers that they receive from the federal government. Total state revenues amounted to around 4 per cent of GDP in 1991, of which around 60 per cent came from revenue sharing transfers. Municipalities' revenues amounted to just over 1 per cent of GDP in 1991, of which around 45 per cent came from transfers. Despite the decentralisation that has taken place, the Mexican government retains a high degree of control over activities at the state and municipal level.

In the National Development Plan for 1995-2000, the Zedillo administration has reaffirmed its commitment to developing a more effective federal structure through its policy of "new federalism". This policy recognises the need for all levels of government to share responsibility for programmes and has the aim of redressing differences in development among states and municipalities through redistribution of resources and opportunities. To do this, functions and programmes will be assigned to states and municipalities according to a criteria of efficiency and equality in the provision of services. The System of Fiscal Co-ordination will also be reviewed jointly by all three levels of government in an endeavour to get a more appropriate distribution of fiscal resources.

As with any major structural reform, achieving a successful redistribution of the functions of government will not be an easy task: identifying in detail the appropriate redistribution of responsibilities and of revenues will require careful study and new arrangements will take time to put into place. This is particularly the case in a country like Mexico where some of the political and administrative structures at the state and municipal levels may be relatively under-developed and less than fully equipped to take on significant new tasks especially in areas where there is a shortage of qualified personnel.

Notes

1. The United Kingdom is a notable exception, having recentralised some activities. See OECD (1992).
2. See Hommes (1995) for a discussion of some of these issues.
3. Following the classification first set out by Musgrave (1959).
4. As has happened in Canada, see OECD (1994*a*). This issue is discussed more generally in Tanzi (1995).
5. These constraints may be self-imposed, as in the United States. Another argument for limiting the borrowing capacity of lower levels is the risk that lower levels will rely on central government to bail them out of any difficulties.
6. See Tiebout (1956).
7. There is some evidence that this has happened in the United States, see Brown and Oates (1987).
8. See Pauly (1973).
9. It could however be argued that redistribution between communities leads to efficiency losses by slowing the migration between communities by providing services to some communities beyond a level justified by the community's longer-term economic outlook. A better use of resources in this circumstance might be to subsidise internal migration rather than continue funding resources to maintain communities as they stand. See Stiglitz (1988).
10. In this case, the costs of monitoring to ensure that the central government's objectives are met may be lower if the government administers the program through its own network of local offices than through locally elected government because locally elected government is not only concerned with acting as an agent of the central government but also with ensuring its own re-election. An alternative option would be for the central government to contract out for the provision of these services through a contestable bidding process, open to all potential suppliers (including local authorities), with the bidding process itself and the contracts designed to provide the incentives for good performance and minimise the monitoring costs.
11. Specific grants that do not have tight conditions attached would, in practice, function in a similar fashion to sectoral block grants.
12. For example, improving the standard of housing may make a bigger contribution to improving health status in a area than building more hospitals.
13. See Musgrave (1983).
14. The outcome of a system with significantly different progressive rates of income taxation in different localities is unstable. A discussion of these issues is presented in Sterks and De Kam (1990).

15. Imposing a surcharge would potentially add to administration and collection costs because more information would be required in calculating different withholding tax rates for residents of different localities, but would retain the economies of scale of centralised collection.
16. This analysis excludes the four smallest OECD countries (Iceland, Ireland, Luxembourg and New Zealand).
17. Excluding employment in public enterprises.
18. See Söderström (1990).
19. See Stiglitz (1988).
20. See Tanzi (1995).
21. This is partly based on Sempere and Sobarzo (1994).
22. Health care for those not covered by the social security institutions (IMSS and ISSSTE).

References

Brown, C. C., and W. E. Oates (1987), "Assistance to the poor in a federal system", *Journal of Public Economics,* Vol. 32, pp. 307-330.

Hommes, R. (1995), "Conflicts and Dilemmas of Decentralisation", *Annual Bank Conference on Development Economics*, The World Bank, Washington.

Musgrave, R. A. (1959), *The Theory of Public Finance*, McGraw-Hill, New York.

Musgrave, R. A. (1983), "Who should tax, where and what?", in C. McClure (ed.), *Tax Assignment in Federal Countries*, Australian National University Press, Canberra.

OECD (1992), *Public Management: OECD Country Profiles*, Paris.

OECD (1994a), *Economic Survey of Canada*, Paris.

OECD (1994b), *Revenue Statistics of OECD Member Countries, 1965-1993*, Paris.

Pauly, M. (1973), "Income redistribution as a local public good", *Journal of Public Economics*, Vol. 12.

Sempere, J. and H. Sobarzo (1994), "Fiscal Decentralisation in Mexico: A Few Proposals", mimeo.

Söderström, L. (1990), "Fiscal Federalism: The Nordic Countries' Style", in R. Prud'homme (ed.), *Public Finance with Several Levels of Government*, Proceedings of the 46th Congress of the International Institute of Public Finance, Brussels.

Sterks, C. M. and C. A. De Kam, (1990), "Decentralising Taxation in the Netherlands", in Prud'homme (ed.).

Stiglitz, J. E. (1988), *Economics of the Public Sector*, 2nd Edition, W. W. Norton and Company.

Tanzi, V. (1995), "Fiscal Federalism and Decentralisation: A Review of Some Efficiency and Macroeconomic Aspects", *Annual Bank Conference on Development Economics*, The World Bank, Washington.

Tiebout, C. (1956), "A pure theory of local expenditures", *Journal of Political Economy*, Vol. 64, pp. 416-424.

Chronology of recent events

1992

June

A US$3 billion road privatisation programme is approved by Congress.

July

Bancen, the last of 18 State banks, is privatised, raising the total revenue from banking privatisation to almost US$13 billion.

October

The maximum rate at which the peso can devalue against the US dollar is raised from 20 to 40 centavos per day – a slide equivalent to 4.6 per cent per annum; this rate applies only to the peso selling rate, while the buying rate continues to be fixed at 3 056 pesos to the US dollar.

November

The government, employers and trade unions renew the Pacto until end-1993.

December

A currency reform reduces the units of the peso by 1 000 in order to create a new peso equivalent to 1 000 old pesos.

1993

June

The OECD Ministerial Council meeting invites Mexico to examine "the terms and conditions of membership with a view towards early entry".

The Canadian House of Commons and Senate vote to ratify the North American Free Trade Agreement (NAFTA).

The two State-owned television networks are privatised.

August

Mexico, Canada and the United States agree to supplemental clauses to NAFTA covering labour and environmental protection.

The Constitution is amended, making the central bank independent and giving it the mandate of preserving price stability.

September

The government sells a majority stake in Asemex, the fourth-largest insurance company, for US$582 million.

October

The government, employers and trade unions renew the Pacto until end-1994. The new Pacto includes increased public investment and tax expenditures to boost the economy out of recession.

A rural development plan (Procampo) is announced, ending price supports for basic grains and introducing direct cash subsidies for farmers according to the amount and fertility of their land.

The government sells Miconsa, the second-largest cornflour producer, for US$140 million.

November

The US House of Representatives and the Mexican Senate approve NAFTA.

Mexico is admitted as new member of the Asia Pacific Economic Co-operation (APEC) grouping.

December

Mexico concludes a free trade agreement with Colombia and Venezuela.

1994

January

A rebellion breaks down in the Southern state of Chiapas in coincidence with the entry into force of NAFTA.

March

Luís Donaldo Colosio, presidential candidate of the ruling PRI party, is assassinated.

Mexico and Costa Rica conclude a free trade agreement, to take effect from January 1, 1995.

April

Mexico is formally accepted as a member of the OECD.

New financial regulations introduced after NAFTA allow banks, brokerages, insurance and other financial institutions based in the United States and Canada to open subsidiaries in Mexico.

May

The government sells its final stake in Telmex in a convertible offering worth up to US$550 million. Receipts are to be placed in the special contingency fund.

June

Manuel Camacho Solis, head of the Commission for Peace and Reconciliation in Chiapas, resigns.

August

Ernesto Zedillo Ponce de León, candidate of the ruling PRI party, is elected President.

Mexico and Bolivia conclude a free trade agreement, to take effect from January 1 1995.

September

The government, the central bank, employers and trade unions renew the Pacto until end-1995. The new Pacto leaves exchange rate policy unchanged and includes tax breaks aimed at stimulating investment rather than consumption.

José Francisco Ruiz Massieu, the PRI secretary-general, is assassinated.

October

Intervention by the government in two large banks (Unión and Cremi).

December

Ernesto Zedillo is sworn in as new President. In his acceptance speech, he promises to uphold the rule of the law by guaranteeing the independence of the judiciary and ensuring the separation of the government from the PRI. A senior official from the conservative opposition National Action Party (PAN) is named Attorney General.

The rebel Zapatista National Liberation Army (EZLN) resumes guerrilla activity in Chiapas.

The peso comes under speculative attacks on financial markets. On December 20, the currency is devaluated by 15 per cent, followed two days later by the decision to let the peso float freely. Finance minister Jaime Serra Puche resigns.

On December 28 the government and the EZLN reach an agreement to end military operations and to begin peace negotiations.

1995

January

The Agreement to Overcome the Economic Emergency is signed by the social partners. The economic programme is announced, which aims at tightening monetary policy, reducing government spending and accelerating privatisations.

A US$50 billion financial rescue package is prepared by the United States and Canadian governments, the International Monetary Funds and the Bank for International Settlements. In addition, the World Bank announces its readiness to commit US$2 billion in 1995. In return to this financial assistance, the Mexican government agrees to a series of conditions, including tight targets for monetary and fiscal policies and for privatisation revenues, further structural reforms, publicity for key fiscal and financial data and the channeling of proceeds from oil exports to a special account at the Federal Reserve Bank of New York.

February

The PAN candidate wins the gubernatorial race in the state of Jalisco, while the PRI keeps the state of Tabasco.

The Bank of Mexico unveils a series of measures designed to stabilise financial markets, including a programme to index loan payments to inflation, a five-year programme (PROCAPTE) aimed at boosting the capitalisation ratio of participating banks and the creation of a futures market for the peso.

Raúl Salinas de Gortari, the elder brother of the former president, is arrested and charged with masterminding the assasination of Ruiz Massieu.

March

The government announces a new package of measures in the wake of continuing peso depreciation. This includes more stringent targets for net credit creation, a further tightening of government spending, an increase in the VAT base rate and an adjustment of public tariffs.

The government takes over the management of Grupo Financiero Asemex-Banpaís, which owns the eigth-largest bank and the fourth-largest insurance company.

April

A bill is approved that allows private companies to distribute natural gas in Mexico, eliminating the monopoly of PEMEX.

The Chicago Mercantile Exchange begins trading futures on the dollar per peso exchange rate.

The Telecommunications Act, approved by Congress, sets the framework for a fully-competitive market environment.

The Air Transport Law sets the basis for opening up the sector.

May

The Chamber of Deputies approves a bill that will introduce competition in the market for wireless telecommunication services.

The PAN candidate wins the gubernatorial race in the state of Guanajato, while the PRI keeps the state of Yucatan.

President Zedillo releases the new administration's six-year National Development Plan.

June

Banco Bilbao Vizcaya takes control of Probursa, the first Mexican bank to be acquired by a foreign bank.

STATISTICAL ANNEX AND STRUCTURAL INDICATORS

Table A. **Selected background statistics**

	Average 1985-94	1985	1986	1987	1988	1989	1990	1991	1992	1993	1994[1]
A. Percentage changes from previous year at constant 1980 prices											
Private consumption	2.8	3.6	-2.8	-0.1	1.8	6.8	6.1	4.9	3.9	0.2	3.7
Gross fixed asset formation	4.5	7.9	-11.8	-0.1	5.8	6.4	13.1	8.3	10.8	-1.2	8.1
Private sector	7.5	12.2	-10.4	6.4	10.3	7.5	13.3	13.0	15.8	1.2	8.0
Public sector	-2.1	0.9	-14.2	-12.2	-4.2	3.6	12.7	-4.4	-5.0	-3.8	8.9
GDP	2.0	2.8	-3.8	1.9	1.2	3.3	4.4	3.6	2.8	0.7	3.5
GDP price deflator	42.6	56.5	73.6	139.7	99.5	25.8	29.5	21.6	14.6	10.0	7.4
Industrial production	2.6	4.8	-5.6	3.3	2.4	5.5	5.7	3.4	3.1	0.2	4.0
Employment[2]	1.0	2.2	-1.4	1.0	0.9	1.3	0.9	2.6	0.4	0.2	1.6
Compensation of employees[2]	-3.9	-8.6	-9.3	-8.4	-11.9	-5.3	-5.0	-1.5	8.7	1.6	2.5
Productivity (GDP/employment)[2]	1.0	0.6	-2.3	0.8	0.4	2.1	3.5	1.0	1.6	0.7	1.9
Unit labour cost (compensation/GDP)[2]	-5.8	-11.1	-5.8	-10.0	-12.9	-8.4	-9.1	-5.0	6.5	0.7	-1.0
B. Percentage ratios											
Gross fixed capital formation as % of GDP at constant prices	18.6	17.9	16.4	16.1	16.8	17.3	18.7	19.6	21.1	20.7	21.6
Stockbuilding as % of GDP at constant prices	0.2	0.4	-1.1	-0.2	0.7	0.5	0.1	-0.0	0.7	0.4	0.4
Foreign balance as % of GDP at constant prices	5.4	7.7	9.5	10.5	8.7	6.8	4.9	3.4	0.5	1.4	0.5
Compensation of employees as % of GDP at current prices	27.1	28.7	28.5	26.8	26.2	25.7	25.0	25.8	27.3	28.5	28.8
Unemployment as % of labour force[3]	3.4	4.4	4.3	3.9	3.5	2.9	2.7	2.6	2.8	3.4	3.7
C. Other indicator											
Current balance (US$ billion)	-10.4	0.8	-1.4	4.2	-2.4	-5.8	-7.4	-14.9	-24.4	-23.4	-28.8

1. Preliminary figures.
2. National accounts data.
3. National Survey of Urban Employment.
Source: OECD.

Table B. Gross domestic product and expenditure

Million new pesos, constant 1980 prices

	1984	1985	1986	1987	1988	1989	1990	1991	1992	1993	1994
Private consumption	2 977	3 075	2 995	2 991	3 046	3 252	3 450	3 619	3 761	3 767	3 907
Public consumption	553	558	566	559	556	556	569	591	605	617	632
Gross fixed asset formation	817	881	777	776	821	874	988	1 070	1 187	1 172	1 267
Public	315	318	273	240	229	238	268	256	243	234	255
Private construction	283	305	285	311	307	328	334	361	411	438	461
Machinery and equipment	284	329	280	270	321	358	435	500	574	572	630
Stockbuilding	–8	18	–48	–7	41	27	12	5	41	24	22
Total domestic demand	4 339	4 531	4 291	4 320	4 464	4 708	5 018	5 285	5 593	5 579	5 828
Exports of goods and services	789	754	788	862	912	933	967	1 011	1 027	1 067	1 145
Imports of goods and services	331	367	339	357	488	592	709	827	1 000	988	1 115
Foreign balance	458	387	448	506	424	341	258	184	27	79	30
Gross domestic product	4 797	4 918	4 739	4 825	4 888	5 049	5 277	5 469	5 620	5 659	5 857

Source: OECD.

165

Table C. Gross domestic product and expenditure

Million new pesos, current prices

	1984	1985	1986	1987	1988	1989	1990	1991	1992	1993	1994
Private consumption	18 590	30 575	54 209	127 268	270 998	356 900	486 354	621 208	735 865	805 684	891 199
Public consumption	2 722	4 374	7 208	16 995	33 741	42 915	57 798	77 971	102 751	121 952	147 314
Gross fixed asset formation	5 287	9 048	15 415	35 667	75 199	92 220	127 728	168 486	211 934	229 541	258 835
Public	1 946	3 147	5 176	10 071	19 717	24 474	33 517	39 401	42 899	45 899	54 233
Private construction	1 651	2 771	4 635	11 764	24 285	29 653	37 381	51 530	69 335	68 243	..
Machinery and equipment	2 197	4 003	7 098	16 101	35 067	44 144	63 882	85 623	107 678	106 165	..
Stockbuilding	566	987	-734	1 566	4 501	16 480	22 544	25 327	25 254	18 289	15 845
Total domestic demand	27 164	44 984	76 098	181 496	384 439	508 515	694 425	892 993	1 075 802	1 175 466	1 313 193
Exports of goods and services	5 122	7 305	13 732	37 692	65 568	81 148	108 299	119 535	128 325	139 948	161 624
Imports of goods and services	2 815	4 897	10 639	25 877	59 555	82 045	116 318	147 363	184 972	187 831	225 925
Foreign balance	2 307	2 408	3 094	11 816	6 012	-897	-8 019	-27 828	-56 646	-47 882	-65 789
Gross domestic product	29 472	47 392	79 191	193 312	390 451	507 618	686 406	865 166	1 019 156	1 127 584	1 248 892

Source: OECD.

Table D. Gross domestic product by industry of origin

Million new pesos, current prices

	1984	1985	1986	1987	1988	1989	1990	1991	1992	1993	1994
Agriculture, forestry and fishing	2 464	4 082	7 062	16 676	33 966	44 230	63 277	78 450	86 716	94 004	101 392
Mining and quarrying	1 662	2 218	2 899	9 810	12 753	13 595	17 696	18 120	21 424	19 708	21 344
Manufacturing	6 618	11 069	19 446	49 551	105 403	124 087	156 180	192 527	215 711	226 843	250 543
Construction	1 298	2 070	3 383	7 887	15 726	19 588	27 230	36 217	48 491	59 426	66 750
Electricity, gas and water	282	449	994	2 090	4 959	6 785	9 480	13 068	15 721	17 276	18 739
Wholesale and retail trade, hotels and restaurants	8 362	13 306	21 185	52 425	106 622	135 438	178 783	214 150	244 150	254 772	280 228
Transportation, storage and communication	2 004	3 165	5 708	13 767	29 528	37 610	56 505	76 545	95 105	109 010	127 158
Financial services, insurance and real estate	2 234	3 531	6 218	13 761	30 663	52 804	80 973	108 410	136 127	163 271	185 122
Community services	4 834	7 831	12 918	29 725	59 839	81 472	112 301	150 462	194 880	234 912	261 362
Total industries	29 757	47 721	79 813	195 691	399 461	515 608	702 424	887 948	1 058 325	1 179 223	1 312 637
Gross domestic product	29 472	47 392	79 191	193 312	390 451	507 618	686 406	865 166	1 019 156	1 127 584	1 248 892

Source: OECD.

167

Table E. **Cost components of GDP**

	1984	1985	1986	1987	1988	1989	1990	1991	1992	1993
Million new pesos										
Compensation of employees	8 445	13 590	22 605	51 878	102 179	130 490	171 415	222 960	278 554	320 854
Operating surplus	15 293	24 043	39 396	97 421	205 898	275 701	382 538	473 395	539 515	585 828
Consumption of fixed capital	3 359	5 331	10 871	25 284	46 763	53 637	66 239	82 703	98 237	112 881
Indirect taxes	3 164	5 688	8 541	23 523	42 548	56 245	74 873	93 852	111 889	118 837
less Subsidies	789	1 261	2 222	4 795	6 937	8 455	8 660	7 743	9 039	10 816
Gross domestic product	29 472	47 392	79 191	193 312	390 451	507 618	686 406	865 166	1 019 156	1 127 584
Per cent of GDP										
Compensation of employees	28.7	28.7	28.5	26.8	26.2	25.7	25.0	25.8	27.3	28.5
Operating surplus	51.9	50.7	49.7	50.4	52.7	54.3	55.7	54.7	52.9	52.0
Consumption of fixed capital	11.4	11.2	13.7	13.1	12.0	10.6	9.7	9.6	9.6	10.0
Indirect taxes	10.7	12.0	10.8	12.2	10.9	11.1	10.9	10.8	11.0	10.5
less Subsidies	2.7	2.7	2.8	2.5	1.8	1.7	1.3	0.9	0.9	1.0

Source: OECD.

168

Table F. **Prices and real wages**

	1985	1986	1987	1988	1989	1990	1991	1992	1993	1994[1]
Real earning by occupied person[2] (1988 = 100)										
Total	123.5	111.9	109.7	100.0	105.1	108.0	111.6	120.2	126.0	..
Agriculture	125.6	126.1	117.3	100.0	95.6	91.5	84.8	82.5	80.9	..
Manufacturing	110.1	101.4	100.5	100.0	106.7	110.4	116.3	126.1	131.0	140.9
Construction	132.1	118.0	113.9	100.0	95.5	94.9	96.7	100.7	103.8	126.8
Commerce, hotels et restaurants	132.6	119.8	113.0	100.0	103.1	102.6	104.9	106.9	112.1	..
Federal government	130.4	109.5	111.6	100.0	111.5	116.6	124.6	141.1	153.6	..
Prices (annual % changes)										
Deflators										
Gross domestic product	56.5	73.6	139.7	99.5	25.8	29.5	21.6	14.6	10.0	7.4
Private consumption	58.8	82.5	135.1	109.1	23.3	28.5	21.8	14.0	9.3	6.6
Exports of goods and services	49.3	78.0	150.7	64.5	21.0	28.8	5.5	5.6	5.1	7.6
Imports of goods and services	56.7	135.1	131.3	68.3	13.6	18.4	8.5	3.9	2.8	6.5
Terms of trade	-4.8	-24.3	8.4	-2.3	6.5	8.8	-2.7	1.7	2.2	1.0
Producer prices	55.2	79.5	145.3	99.3	12.8	22.7	19.1	12.0	6.6	6.4
Consumer prices[3]	63.7	105.7	159.2	51.7	19.7	29.9	18.8	11.9	8.0	7.1
Basic basket[4]	61.3	125.3	155.9	41.6	15.4	33.6	22.3	8.1	7.5	8.1
Other goods and services	65.1	94.8	161.3	58.0	22.1	27.9	16.8	14.1	8.3	6.5

1. Provisional.
2. Deflated by the consumer price index.
3. December to December
4. Basic goods and services, of which some supplied by the public sector (gasoline, electricity).
Source: INEGI.

Table G. Federal government revenue and expenditure

Million new pesos

	1984	1985	1986	1987	1988	1989	1990	1991	1992	1993	1994 [1]
Total revenue	4 975	7 991	12 670	32 974	68 015	90 204	117 710	147 458	210 446	194 813	213 467
Tax revenue	4 744	7 578	11 902	30 891	60 757	78 872	105 206	134 724	161 002	178 016	191 152
Direct taxes	2 921	4 664	6 345	17 818	32 918	43 894	59 070	75 419	92 418	104 254	102 845
PEMEX	1 708	2 741	2 980	10 163	13 451	17 985	26 098	31 215	34 473	35 033	31 124
Income tax	1 213	1 923	3 365	7 655	19 468	25 909	32 972	44 205	57 945	69 221	71 721
Indirect taxes	1 823	2 914	5 557	13 073	27 839	34 978	46 136	59 305	68 584	73 762	88 307
VAT	943	1 478	2 498	6 266	14 024	17 024	26 636	32 533	30 452	33 125	39 080
Excise taxes	662	1 023	2 188	4 862	10 888	12 632	11 203	11 496	18 190	19 317	27 904
Gasoline	450	678	1 497	3 277	7 277	7 987	5 163	6 951	12 669	13 400	21 787
Other	212	345	690	1 585	3 611	4 645	6 039	4 545	5 521	5 918	6 117
Import duties	141	302	632	1 472	1 741	3 755	6 312	9 749	12 687	12 544	12 677
Other taxes	78	111	240	474	1 187	1 567	1 985	5 527	7 255	8 776	8 647
Non-tax revenue	231	413	768	2 082	7 258	11 333	12 505	12 734	49 444	16 797	22 315
Total expenditure	7 107	11 573	23 012	60 440	105 857	115 795	137 147	147 419	163 920	185 189	221 202
Current expenditure	6 156	9 780	20 514	54 241	98 325	105 864	118 881	125 964	139 018	162 864	191 288
Wages, acquisitions, general services and other services	1 159	1 824	3 124	7 364	13 400	18 476	22 523	33 086	28 322	34 999	42 277
Interest	2 159	4 217	11 168	34 463	60 919	59 752	59 917	43 354	36 514	28 870	27 097
Participations and transfers	2 162	3 417	5 332	11 503	22 197	27 198	34 366	47 714	71 964	96 747	118 829
Other [2]	676	322	890	911	1 809	438	2 075	1 810	2 217	2 249	3 085
Capital expenditure	951	1 793	2 498	6 199	7 532	9 931	18 266	21 456	24 903	22 325	29 914
Investment	263	451	860	1 864	2 228	2 934	5 775	8 360	10 729	12 159	16 972
Capital transfers	540	1 077	1 521	4 201	4 934	6 522	11 395	9 249	12 749	8 707	11 046
Other [2]	148	265	117	134	370	475	1 096	3 847	1 425	1 458	1 896

1. Preliminary figures.
2. Includes other current transfers, deferred payments and savings.
Source: Ministry of Finance.

Table H. **Public enterprises under budgetary control** [1]

Million new pesos

	1984	1985	1986	1987	1988	1989	1990	1991	1992	1993	1994
Budgetary revenues	5 251	8 162	12 863	28 293	53 947	58 340	80 192	85 210	95 649	110 750	123 858
PEMEX	2 136	2 723	4 154	8 834	16 491	16 790	25 672	25 588	26 405	27 905	30 933
Public enterprises excluding PEMEX	2 113	3 673	6 419	15 303	31 452	33 793	45 475	52 143	61 028	67 716	75 297
Transfers	1 002	1 766	2 290	4 156	6 004	7 757	9 045	7 479	8 215	15 129	17 629
Budgetary expenditures	5 010	7 943	13 197	28 165	52 083	59 163	77 271	86 344	97 381	106 360	118 961
Current expenditures	4 031	6 574	11 009	22 897	42 206	47 908	62 463	67 628	77 953	86 855	94 185
Wages and salaries	815	1 408	2 343	5 260	9 976	11 983	16 072	20 967	27 135	30 055	33 574
Interest payments	1 091	1 337	2 221	3 912	6 019	7 358	7 201	4 865	4 333	4 463	5 691
Goods and services	2 036	3 656	6 096	13 076	25 118	28 297	36 202	37 743	44 408	50 481	54 920
Other expenditures	89	173	349	649	1 093	270	2 988	4 053	2 078	1 856	0
Capital expenditures	979	1 369	2 188	5 268	9 877	11 255	14 808	18 716	19 428	19 505	24 776
Investment	973	1 336	2 074	5 190	9 787	11 221	14 403	18 122	18 466	18 806	20 313
Other	6	33	114	78	90	34	405	594	962	699	4 463

1. Including social security and other agencies.
Source: Ministry of Finance.

171

Table I. **Summary of the financial system**

Million new pesos

	1984	1985	1986	1987	1988	1989	1990	1991	1992	1993	1994
Bank of Mexico											
Net international reserves	1 233	1 095	2 676	19 186	4 147	1 953	12 271	35 989	41 926	64 440	15 040
Net domestic assets	-114	637	383	-11 868	9 012	16 039	12 332	-3 573	-3 914	-21 212	36 830
Net credit to public sector	3 746	5 735	9 863	9 866	31 465	38 053	40 070	21 413	15 450	-9 404	-1 093
Credit to private sector	44	90	239	587	602	722	855	1 060	1 327	1 456	2 364
Other (net)	-3 904	-5 188	-9 719	-22 321	-23 055	-22 736	-28 593	-26 046	-20 691	-13 264	35 559
Note issue	1 119	1 732	3 059	7 318	13 159	17 992	24 603	32 416	38 012	43 228	51 870
Financial system											
Net foreign assets	1 897	2 927	8 187	36 167	18 934	23 218	30 884	47 671	54 648	67 933	26 180
Net domestic credit	14 489	25 270	56 732	122 915	171 558	224 337	277 882	359 251	430 000	501 065	789 115
Net credit to public sector	9 424	17 885	43 078	90 899	116 540	135 851	142 427	139 602	102 429	62 256	130 128
Net Credit to private sector	4 196	6 670	11 480	29 189	53 395	94 966	149 534	233 811	346 174	434 992	617 440
Other (net)	869	715	2 174	2 827	1 623	-6 481	-14 079	-14 162	-18 603	3 817	41 547
Medium and long-term foreign obligations	6 827	13 649	36 034	90 541	90 930	106 853	110 321	124 747	133 801	150 270	293 125
Liabilities to nonbank financial intermediaries	903	1 832	4 269	10 705	16 562	21 500	26 743	29 247	32 859	48 862	75 102
Liabilities to private sector	8 657	12 716	24 617	57 836	82 999	119 201	171 702	252 928	317 988	369 866	447 068
Monetary aggregates (% of GDP)											
M2	30.4	27.7	32.2	31.8	22.4	24.6	26.6	31.1	31.8	32.9	36.3
M4	35.3	33.3	41.2	43.7	34.4	39.9	43.2	44.8	45.6	52.5	59.9
Interest rate											
3-month Cetes rate	49.65	63.69	88.71	102.83	63.98	44.77	35.03	19.82	15.89	15.50	14.68

Source: Bank of Mexico.

Table J. **Balance of payments, OECD basis**

Million dollars

	1984	1985	1986	1987	1988	1989	1990	1991	1992	1993
Exports, f.o.b	24 196	21 664	16 158	20 495	20 547	22 842	26 838	26 855	27 516	30 033
Imports, f.o.b	12 167	14 534	12 433	13 306	20 273	25 438	31 271	38 184	48 193	48 924
Trade balance	12 029	7 130	3 725	7 189	274	-2 596	-4 433	-11 329	-20 677	-18 891
Services, net	-9 206	-8 314	-6 676	-4 861	-4 903	-5 772	-6 993	-6 305	-7 150	-7 187
Balance on goods and services	2 823	-1 184	-2 951	2 328	-4 629	-8 368	-11 426	-17 634	-27 827	-26 078
Current balance	4 183	800	-1 377	4 247	-2 374	-5 825	-7 451	-14 888	-24 806	-23 391
Long-term capital, net	3 995	1 670	1 414	3 434	-1 892	2 435	5 679	21 816	20 160	31 450
Private	-4 813	-9 915	-6 928	-676	2 225	2 536	3 994	23 283	25 598	32 615
Official	8 808	11 585	8 342	4 110	-4 117	-101	1 685	-1 467	-5 438	-1 165
Basic balance	8 178	2 470	37	7 681	-4 266	-3 390	-1 772	6 928	-4 646	8 059
Non-monetary short-term capital	-6 297	-5 141	133	-1 457	-2 464	4 064	802	-873	5 126	-2 184
Private	-4 174	-2 225	646	-4 181	723	-436	-399	1 392	6 011	-777
Official	-8	1	226	-229	5	-3	-28	13	-429	29
Errors and omissions	-2 115	-2 917	-739	2 953	-3 192	4 503	1 229	-2 278	-456	-1 436
Balance on non-monetary capital	1 881	-2 671	170	6 224	-6 730	674	-970	6 055	480	5 875
Monetary capital, net	268	-58	-288	-641	93	-497	3 274	1 938	1 266	1 357
Assets	69	-105	-342	-888	-324	-494	-676	-1 156	26	-1 283
Liabilities	199	47	54	247	417	-3	3 950	3 094	1 240	2 640
Balance on non-monetary and monetary transactions	2 149	-2 729	-118	5 583	-6 637	177	2 304	7 993	1 746	7 232
Use of fund credit	1 241	295	712	402	-83	365	958	160	-572	-1 175
Change in reserves	3 391	-2 434	595	5 985	-6 722	542	3 261	8 154	1 173	6 057
Gold	-188	-47	112	-47	18	-611	-268	282	-98	-39
Currency assets	3 691	-2 384	477	5 384	-6 459	1 152	3 532	7 700	1 300	6 425
Reserve position in the IMF	-93	0	0	0	0	0	0	0	0	0
Special drawing rights	-19	-3	6	648	-281	1	-3	172	-29	-329

Source: OECD; Bank of Mexico.

173

Table K. **Foreign trade by commodity group**

Million dollars

	1984	1985	1986	1987	1988	1989	1990	1991	1992	1993	1994[1]
Total exports	25 351	22 932	17 452	22 093	22 882	25 849	30 390	30 905	32 259	35 443	40 340
Total merchandise exports	24 196	21 664	16 157	20 495	20 545	22 842	26 838	26 855	27 516	30 033	34 564
Agriculture, forestry and fishing	1 461	1 409	2 098	1 543	1 670	1 754	2 162	2 373	2 112	2 504	2 678
Mining	539	510	510	576	660	605	617	547	356	278	357
Petroleum	16 601	14 767	6 307	8 630	6 711	7 876	10 104	8 166	8 307	7 418	7 393
Manufactures[2]	5 595	4 978	7 242	9 746	11 504	12 607	13 955	15 769	16 740	19 832	24 136
Food, beverages and tobacco	822	751	937	1 313	1 363	1 268	1 095	1 216	1 131	1 363	..
Textiles, clothing and leather	275	195	333	566	619	623	632	764	889	981	..
Chemicals	756	674	830	1 093	1 385	1 537	1 679	1 975	2 099	2 117	..
Metal and mineral manufactures	1 177	954	1 292	1 707	2 087	2 466	2 409	2 382	2 385	2 817	..
Automobiles, motors and parts	1 580	1 572	2 450	3 187	3 481	3 882	4 790	5 272	6 091	7 301	..
Machinery and equipment, electronics	590	506	885	1 159	1 589	1 855	2 276	2 761	3 276	4 325	..
Other manufactures	395	326	515	721	980	976	1 074	1 399	869	928	..
In-bond industries (maquiladoras), net	1 155	1 268	1 295	1 598	2 337	3 007	3 551	4 051	4 743	5 410	5 776
Total merchandise imports	12 167	14 534	12 433	13 306	20 273	25 438	31 271	38 184	48 193	48 924	58 882
Agriculture, forestry and fishing	1 880	1 607	938	1 108	1 773	2 003	2 071	2 130	2 827	2 593	3 338
Manufactures	10 035	12 582	11 202	11 854	18 119	22 831	28 523	35 473	44 344	45 711	54 845
Food, beverages and tobacco	500	508	490	460	1 233	2 014	2 679	2 584	3 279	3 313	..
Chemicals, petroleum derivatives	2 121	2 703	2 133	2 392	3 049	3 823	4 159	5 080	5 930	6 342	..
Metallurgy, steel and mineral products	1 078	1 222	915	971	1 659	2 004	2 330	3 130	3 811	3 524	..
Metal products, machinery and equipment	5 615	7 242	6 732	6 872	10 248	12 250	15 963	20 212	25 760	26 117	..
Other manufactures	721	907	932	1 159	1 930	2 740	3 392	4 467	5 564	6 414	..
Other	252	345	292	344	381	604	678	618	1 021	620	700

1. Preliminary figures.
2. Not including petrochemicals and petroleum derivatives which are included here in petroleum exports.
Source: INEGI.

174

Table L. Foreign trade by area
Million dollars[1]

	1985	1986	1987	1988	1989	1990	1991	1992	1993	1994[2]
	Exports, f.o.b									
Total	21 664	16 158	20 494	20 546	22 842	26 838	42 688	46 196	51 886	60 833
OECD countries	19 424	14 205	18 153	17 924	20 364	24 234	39 861	42 859	48 232	57 334
USA	13 158	10 627	13 361	13 556	15 924	18 456	33 953	37 468	43 116	51 894
Canada	400	191	316	278	277	458	1 125	1 000	1 541	1 470
Japan	1 719	1 057	1 348	1 231	1 314	1 506	1 241	793	700	988
EEC	4 044	2 173	2 970	2 691	2 663	3 513	3 292	3 299	2 600	2 713
Non-OECD countries	2 126	1 769	2 336	2 617	2 363	2 524	2 760	3 315	3 632	3 450
Asia[3]	270	303	410	500	328	324	325	321	436	414
Latin America	1 197	1 108	1 437	1 449	1 398	1 514	1 756	2 244	2 597	2 579
	Imports, f.o.b									
Total	14 533	12 433	13 305	20 274	25 438	31 272	49 967	62 129	65 367	79 375
OECD countries	11 897	10 592	11 417	17 434	21 484	28 263	46 087	56 827	59 514	72 188
USA	8 675	7 432	7 905	12 631	15 867	20 521	36 868	44 279	46 465	56 942
Canada	238	223	355	338	421	458	670	1 052	1 163	1 600
Japan	735	683	794	1 125	1 081	1 470	1 783	3 041	3 369	3 812
EEC	1 801	1 826	1 980	2 783	3 393	4 773	5 712	7 155	7 288	8 495
Non-OECD countries	932	675	645	1 366	1 890	2 988	3 736	4 875	5 837	7 115
Asia[3]	152	155	180	482	760	1 078	1 523	2 199	2 889	3 574
Latin America	621	387	350	681	895	1 558	1 865	2 228	2 339	2 745

1. Including maquiladoras as from 1991.
2. Provisional data.
3. Excluding Middle East.
Source: INEGI.

Table M. Production structure and performance indicators

A. Production structure

	Per cent share of GDP at current prices				Per cent share of total employment			
	1980	1985	1990	1993	1980	1985	1990	1993
Agriculture, forestry and fishing	8.2	9.1	8.0	6.8	28.0	27.8	25.4	25.5
Mining	3.2	4.6	2.6	1.7	1.0	1.1	1.2	1.1
Manufactures	22.0	23.4	22.8	20.1	12.1	11.2	11.2	10.0
Food, beverages and tobacco	5.4	6.1	5.9	5.8	3.0	3.0	3.0	3.0
Textiles, clothing	3.0	2.6	2.2	1.6	2.2	1.9	1.8	1.5
Wood and wood products	0.9	0.9	0.8	0.6	0.7	0.6	0.5	0.5
Paper and paper products	1.2	1.3	1.4	1.2	0.6	0.6	0.6	0.5
Chemicals, rubber and plastic products	3.3	4.2	4.3	3.7	1.4	1.5	1.6	1.3
Non-metallic minerals	1.5	1.7	1.6	1.7	0.8	0.8	0.8	0.7
Basic metal products	1.4	1.3	1.4	0.9	0.5	0.5	0.4	0.3
Machinery and equipment	4.7	4.8	4.7	4.3	2.8	2.3	2.4	2.1
Other manufacturing	0.6	0.4	0.4	0.4	0.1	0.1	0.2	0.2
Construction	6.4	4.4	4.0	5.3	9.5	8.9	10.7	11.7
Electricity, gas and water	1.0	0.9	1.4	1.5	0.4	0.5	0.5	0.5
Commerce, restaurants and hotels	28.0	28.1	26.0	22.6	14.5	14.3	15.0	14.9
Transportation and communication	6.4	6.7	8.2	9.7	4.5	4.7	4.8	4.9
Financial services, insurance and real estate	8.6	7.7	12.1	14.9	1.8	2.2	2.3	2.3
Community services	17.2	9.3	9.7	12.1	16.3	14.6	13.8	13.7

B. Manufacturing sector performance

	Productivity growth by sector, real GDP/employment (annual rate)		
	1980/1970	1990/1980	1993/1990
Food, beverages and tobacco	2.4	1.2	2.3
Textiles, clothing	2.8	0.6	0.6
Wood and wood products	2.2	1.7	1.7
Paper and paper products	3.8	2.2	1.6
Chemicals, rubber and plastic products	5.5	1.8	5.5
Non-metallic minerals	4.3	0.5	7.1
Basic metal products	2.2	4.1	12.7
Machinery and equipment	3.6	2.2	8.2

Source: OECD.

Table N. **Labour market indicators**

	A. Labour market performance					
	1986	1990	1991	1992	1993	1994
Unemployment rate[1]						
Total	4.3	2.8	2.6	2.8	3.4	3.7
Male	3.7	2.5	2.5	2.6	3.2	3.6
Female	5.3	3.1	2.9	3.2	3.9	3.9
Dispersion of regional unemployment rates[2]	1.55	0.83	1.34	1.31	1.57	1.52

	B. Structural and institutional characteristics				
	1960	1970	1980	1990	1994
Participation rate[3]					
Total	46.5	43.6[4]	50.9	51.8	54.6
Male	78.7	71.7	75.1	72.0	74.5
Female	15.4	16.4	27.8	33.3	36.5
Age structure (% of total population)					
0-14	44.4	46.2	43.1	37.1	
15-24	18.6	18.8	20.7	20.7	
25-34	13.1	12.1	13.0	13.9	
35-44	9.4	9.2	9.2	10.9	
45-64	11.0	9.9	10.1	12.6	
65 and over	3.4	3.7	3.8	4.7	

	1960	1970	1990	1991	1993
Employment: share in total					
Primary sector	54.5	41.8	23.4	27.0	27.1
Secondary sector	19.1	24.4	28.8	23.2	22.2
Tertiary sector	26.4	33.8	47.8	49.8	50.7

	Percentage changes (Average annual rates)		
	1970/1960	1990/1970	1993/1988
Labour force (12 years and over)			
Employment:			
Total	0.89	3.13	3.21
Primary sector	−1.74	0.19	6.00
Secondary sector	3.39	3.99	−0.65
Tertiary sector	3.43	4.92	3.74

1.   Unemployed persons, 12 years and over in urban areas. Based on National Survey on Urban Employment.
2.   Measured by standard deviation for 16 urban areas (1992, 32 urban areas; 1993, 34 urban areas; 1994, 38 urban areas).
3.   Labour force as a percentage of relevant population group, aged 12 years and over. Based on National Survey on Urban Employment.
4.   Definition not comparable due to change in Census methodology.
Source: INEGI, different surveys and census.

BASIC STATISTICS

BASIC STATISTICS:

INTERNATIONAL COMPARISONS

	Units	Reference period [1]	Australia	A
Population				
Total	Thousands	1992	17 489	7
Inhabitants per sq. km	Number	1992	2	
Net average annual increase over previous 10 years	%	1992	1.4	
Employment				
Civilian employment (CE)[2]	Thousands	1992	7 637	3
Of which: Agriculture	% of CE		5.3	
Industry	% of CE		23.8	
Services	% of CE		71	
Gross domestic product (GDP)				
At current prices and current exchange rates	Bill. US$	1992	296.6	
Per capita	US$		16 959	23
At current prices using current PPPs[3]	Bill. US$	1992	294.5	
Per capita	US$		16 800	18
Average annual volume growth over previous 5 years	%	1992	2	
Gross fixed capital formation (GFCF)	% of GDP	1992	19.7	
Of which: Machinery and equipment	% of GDP		9.3	
Residential construction	% of GDP		5.1	
Average annual volume growth over previous 5 years	%	1992	−1	
Gross saving ratio[4]	% of GDP	1992	15.6	
General government				
Current expenditure on goods and services	% of GDP	1992	18.5	
Current disbursements[5]	% of GDP	1992	36.9	
Current receipts	% of GDP	1992	33.1	
Net official development assistance	% of GNP	1992	0.33	
Indicators of living standards				
Private consumption per capita using current PPPs[3]	US$	1992	10 527	9
Passenger cars, per 1 000 inhabitants	Number	1990	430	
Telephones, per 1 000 inhabitants	Number	1990	448	
Television sets, per 1 000 inhabitants	Number	1989	484	
Doctors, per 1 000 inhabitants	Number	1991	2	
Infant mortality per 1 000 live births	Number	1991	7.1	
Wages and prices (average annual increase over previous 5 years)				
Wages (earnings or rates according to availability)	%	1992	5	
Consumer prices	%	1992	5.2	
Foreign trade				
Exports of goods, fob*	Mill. US$	1992	42 844	44
As % of GDP	%		14.4	2
Average annual increase over previous 5 years	%		10.1	
Imports of goods, cif*	Mill. US$	1992	40 751	54
As % of GDP	%		13.7	
Average annual increase over previous 5 years	%		8.6	
Total official reserves[6]	Mill. SDRs	1992	8 152	9
As ratio of average monthly imports of goods	Ratio		2.4	

* At current prices and exchange rates.
1. Unless otherwise stated.
2. According to the definitions used in OECD *Labour Force Statistics*.
3. PPPs = Purchasing Power Parities.
4. Gross saving = Gross national disposable income minus private and government consumption.
5. Current disbursements = Current expenditure on goods and services plus current transfers and payments of property income.
6. Gold included in reserves is valued at 35 SDRs per ounce. End of year.
7. Including Luxembourg.

EMPLOYMENT OPPORTUNITIES
Economics Department, OECD

The Economics Department of the OECD offers challenging and rewarding opportunities to economists interested in applied policy analysis in an international environment. The Department's concerns extend across the entire field of economic policy analysis, both macroeconomic and microeconomic. Its main task is to provide, for discussion by committees of senior officials from Member countries, documents and papers dealing with current policy concerns. Within this programme of work, three major responsibilities are:

- to prepare regular surveys of the economies of individual Member countries;
- to issue full twice-yearly reviews of the economic situation and prospects of the OECD countries in the context of world economic trends;
- to analyse specific policy issues in a medium-term context for the OECD as a whole, and to a lesser extent for the non-OECD countries.

The documents prepared for these purposes, together with much of the Department's other economic work, appear in published form in the *OECD Economic Outlook, OECD Economic Surveys, OECD Economic Studies* and the Department's *Working Papers* series.

The Department maintains a world econometric model, INTERLINK, which plays an important role in the preparation of the policy analyses and twice-yearly projections. The availability of extensive cross-country data bases and good computer resources facilitates comparative empirical analysis, much of which is incorporated into the model.

The Department is made up of about 80 professional economists from a variety of backgrounds and Member countries. Most projects are carried out by small teams and last from four to eighteen months. Within the Department, ideas and points of view are widely discussed; there is a lively professional interchange, and all professional staff have the opportunity to contribute actively to the programme of work.

Skills the Economics Department is looking for:

a) Solid competence in using the tools of both microeconomic and macroeconomic theory to answer policy questions. Experience indicates that this normally requires the equivalent of a Ph.D. in economics or substantial relevant professional experience to compensate for a lower degree.

b) Solid knowledge of economic statistics and quantitative methods; this includes how to identify data, estimate structural relationships, apply basic techniques of time series analysis, and test hypotheses. It is essential to be able to interpret results sensibly in an economic policy context.

c) A keen interest in and extensive knowledge of policy issues, economic developments and their political/social contexts.

d) Interest and experience in analysing questions posed by policy-makers and presenting the results to them effectively and judiciously. Thus, work experience in government agencies or policy research institutions is an advantage.

e) The ability to write clearly, effectively, and to the point. The OECD is a bilingual organisation with French and English as the official languages. Candidates must have excellent knowledge of one of these languages, and some knowledge of the other. Knowledge of other languages might also be an advantage for certain posts.

f) For some posts, expertise in a particular area may be important, but a successful candidate is expected to be able to work on a broader range of topics relevant to the work of the Department. Thus, except in rare cases, the Department does not recruit narrow specialists.

g) The Department works on a tight time schedule with strict deadlines. Moreover, much of the work in the Department is carried out in small groups. Thus, the ability to work with other economists from a variety of cultural and professional backgrounds, to supervise junior staff, and to produce work on time is important.

General information

The salary for recruits depends on educational and professional background. Positions carry a basic salary from FF 305 700 or FF 377 208 for Administrators (economists) and from FF 438 348 for Principal Administrators (senior economists). This may be supplemented by expatriation and/or family allowances, depending on nationality, residence and family situation. Initial appointments are for a fixed term of two to three years.

Vacancies are open to candidates from OECD Member countries. The Organisation seeks to maintain an appropriate balance between female and male staff and among nationals from Member countries.

For further information on employment opportunities in the Economics Department, contact:

Administrative Unit
Economics Department
OECD
2, rue André-Pascal
75775 PARIS CEDEX 16
FRANCE

E-Mail: compte.esadmin@oecd.org

Applications citing ''ECSUR'', together with a detailed *curriculum vitae* in English or French, should be sent to the Head of Personnel at the above address.

MAIN SALES OUTLETS OF OECD PUBLICATIONS
PRINCIPAUX POINTS DE VENTE DES PUBLICATIONS DE L'OCDE

RGENTINA – ARGENTINE
arlos Hirsch S.R.L.
aleria Güemes, Florida 165, 4° Piso
333 Buenos Aires   Tel. (1) 331.1787 y 331.2391
Telefax: (1) 331.1787

USTRALIA – AUSTRALIE
.A. Information Services
48 Whitehorse Road, P.O.B 163
flitcham, Victoria 3132   Tel. (03) 873.4411
Telefax: (03) 873.5679

AUSTRIA – AUTRICHE
ierold & Co.
iraben 31
Vien I   Tel. (0222) 533.50.14
Telefax: (0222) 512.47.31.29

BELGIUM – BELGIQUE
ean De Lannoy
Avenue du Roi 202 Koningslaan
4-1060 Bruxelles   Tel. (02) 538.51.69/538.08.41
Telefax: (02) 538.08.41

CANADA
Renouf Publishing Company Ltd.
294 Algoma Road
Ottawa, ON K1B 3W8   Tel. (613) 741.4333
Telefax: (613) 741.5439
Stores:
51 Sparks Street
Ottawa, ON K1P 5R1   Tel. (613) 238.8985
211 Yonge Street
Toronto, ON M5B 1M4   Tel. (416) 363.3171
Telefax: (416)363.59.63

Les Éditions La Liberté Inc.
3020 Chemin Sainte-Foy
Sainte-Foy, PQ G1X 3V6   Tel. (418) 658.3763
Telefax: (418) 658.3763

Federal Publications Inc.
165 University Avenue, Suite 701
Toronto, ON M5H 3B8   Tel. (416) 860.1611
Telefax: (416) 860.1608

Les Publications Fédérales
1185 Université
Montréal, QC H3B 3A7   Tel. (514) 954.1633
Telefax: (514) 954.1635

CHINA – CHINE
China National Publications Import
Export Corporation (CNPIEC)
16 Gongti E. Road, Chaoyang District
P.O. Box 88 or 50
Beijing 100704 PR   Tel. (01) 506.6688
Telefax: (01) 506.3101

CHINESE TAIPEI – TAIPEI CHINOIS
Good Faith Worldwide Int'l. Co. Ltd.
9th Floor, No. 118, Sec. 2
Chung Hsiao E. Road
Taipei   Tel. (02) 391.7396/391.7397
Telefax: (02) 394.9176

CZECH REPUBLIC – RÉPUBLIQUE TCHÈQUE
Artia Pegas Press Ltd.
Narodni Trida 25
POB 825
111 21 Praha 1   Tel. 26.65.68
Telefax: 26.20.81

DENMARK – DANEMARK
Munksgaard Book and Subscription Service
35, Nørre Søgade, P.O. Box 2148
DK-1016 København K   Tel. (33) 12.85.70
Telefax: (33) 12.93.87

EGYPT – ÉGYPTE
Middle East Observer
41 Sherif Street
Cairo   Tel. 392.6919
Telefax: 360-6804

FINLAND – FINLANDE
Akateeminen Kirjakauppa
Keskuskatu 1, P.O. Box 128
00100 Helsinki
Subscription Services/Agence d'abonnements :
P.O. Box 23
00371 Helsinki   Tel. (358 0) 121 4416
Telefax: (358 0) 121.4450

FRANCE
OECD/OCDE
Mail Orders/Commandes par correspondance:
2, rue André-Pascal
75775 Paris Cedex 16   Tel. (33-1) 45.24.82.00
Telefax: (33-1) 49.10.42.76
Telex: 640048 OCDE
Internet: Compte.PUBSINQ @ oecd.org
Orders via Minitel, France only/
Commandes par Minitel, France exclusivement :
36 15 OCDE
OECD Bookshop/Librairie de l'OCDE :
33, rue Octave-Feuillet
75016 Paris   Tel. (33-1) 45.24.81.81
(33-1) 45.24.81.67
Documentation Française
29, quai Voltaire
75007 Paris   Tel. 40.15.70.00
Gibert Jeune (Droit-Économie)
6, place Saint-Michel
75006 Paris   Tel. 43.25.91.19
Librairie du Commerce International
10, avenue d'Iéna
75016 Paris   Tel. 40.73.34.60
Librairie Dunod
Université Paris-Dauphine
Place du Maréchal de Lattre de Tassigny
75016 Paris   Tel. (1) 44.05.40.13
Librairie Lavoisier
11, rue Lavoisier
75008 Paris   Tel. 42.65.39.95
Librairie L.G.D.J. - Montchrestien
20, rue Soufflot
75005 Paris   Tel. 46.33.89.85
Librairie des Sciences Politiques
30, rue Saint-Guillaume
75007 Paris   Tel. 45.48.36.02
P.U.F.
49, boulevard Saint-Michel
75005 Paris   Tel. 43.25.83.40
Librairie de l'Université
12a, rue Nazareth
13100 Aix-en-Provence   Tel. (16) 42.26.18.08
Documentation Française
165, rue Garibaldi
69003 Lyon   Tel. (16) 78.63.32.23
Librairie Decitre
29, place Bellecour
69002 Lyon   Tel. (16) 72.40.54.54
Librairie Sauramps
Le Triangle
34967 Montpellier Cedex 2   Tel. (16) 67.58.85.15
Tekefax: (16) 67.58.27.36

GERMANY – ALLEMAGNE
OECD Publications and Information Centre
August-Bebel-Allee 6
D-53175 Bonn   Tel. (0228) 959.120
Telefax: (0228) 959.12.17

GREECE – GRÈCE
Librairie Kauffmann
Mavrokordatou 9
106 78 Athens   Tel. (01) 32.55.321
Telefax: (01) 32.30.320

HONG-KONG
Swindon Book Co. Ltd.
Astoria Bldg. 3F
34 Ashley Road, Tsimshatsui
Kowloon, Hong Kong   Tel. 2376.2062
Telefax: 2376.0685

HUNGARY – HONGRIE
Euro Info Service
Margitsziget, Európa Ház
1138 Budapest   Tel. (1) 111.62.16
Telefax: (1) 111.60.61

ICELAND – ISLANDE
Mál Mog Menning
Laugavegi 18, Pósthólf 392
121 Reykjavik   Tel. (1) 552.4240
Telefax: (1) 562.3523

INDIA – INDE
Oxford Book and Stationery Co.
Scindia House
New Delhi 110001   Tel. (11) 331.5896/5308
Telefax: (11) 332.5993
17 Park Street
Calcutta 700016   Tel. 240832

INDONESIA – INDONÉSIE
Pdii-Lipi
P.O. Box 4298
Jakarta 12042   Tel. (21) 573.34.67
Telefax: (21) 573.34.67

IRELAND – IRLANDE
Government Supplies Agency
Publications Section
4/5 Harcourt Road
Dublin 2   Tel. 661.31.11
Telefax: 475.27.60

ISRAEL
Praedicta
5 Shatner Street
P.O. Box 34030
Jerusalem 91430   Tel. (2) 52.84.90/1/2
Telefax: (2) 52.84.93
R.O.Y. International
P.O. Box 13056
Tel Aviv 61130   Tel. (3) 546 1423
Telefax: (3) 546 1442
Palestinian Authority/Middle East:
INDEX Information Services
P.O.B. 19502
Jerusalem   Tel. (2) 27.12.19
Telefax: (2) 27.16.34

ITALY – ITALIE
Libreria Commissionaria Sansoni
Via Duca di Calabria 1/1
50125 Firenze   Tel. (055) 64.54.15
Telefax: (055) 64.12.57
Via Bartolini 29
20155 Milano   Tel. (02) 36.50.83
Editrice e Libreria Herder
Piazza Montecitorio 120
00186 Roma   Tel. 679.46.28
Telefax: 678.47.51
Libreria Hoepli
Via Hoepli 5
20121 Milano   Tel. (02) 86.54.46
Telefax: (02) 805.28.86
Libreria Scientifica
Dott. Lucio de Biasio 'Aeiou'
Via Coronelli, 6
20146 Milano   Tel. (02) 48.95.45.52
Telefax: (02) 48.95.45.48

JAPAN – JAPON
OECD Publications and Information Centre
Landic Akasaka Building
2-3-4 Akasaka, Minato-ku
Tokyo 107   Tel. (81.3) 3586.2016
Telefax: (81.3) 3584.7929

KOREA – CORÉE
Kyobo Book Centre Co. Ltd.
P.O. Box 1658, Kwang Hwa Moon
Seoul   Tel. 730.78.91
Telefax: 735.00.30

MALAYSIA – MALAISIE
University of Malaya Bookshop
University of Malaya
P.O. Box 1127, Jalan Pantai Baru
59700 Kuala Lumpur
Malaysia   Tel. 756.5000/756.5425
                            Telefax: 756.3246

MEXICO – MEXIQUE
Revistas y Periodicos Internacionales S.A. de C.V.
Florencia 57 - 1004
Mexico, D.F. 06600   Tel. 207.81.00
                           Telefax: 208.39.79

NETHERLANDS – PAYS-BAS
SDU Uitgeverij Plantijnstraat
Externe Fondsen
Postbus 20014
2500 EA's-Gravenhage   Tel. (070) 37.89.880
Voor bestellingen: Telefax: (070) 34.75.778

**NEW ZEALAND
NOUVELLE-ZÉLANDE**
GPLegislation Services
P.O. Box 12418
Thorndon, Wellington   Tel. (04) 496.5655
                           Telefax: (04) 496.5698

NORWAY – NORVÈGE
Narvesen Info Center – NIC
Bertrand Narvesens vei 2
P.O. Box 6125 Etterstad
0602 Oslo 6   Tel. (022) 57.33.00
                          Telefax: (022) 68.19.01

PAKISTAN
Mirza Book Agency
65 Shahrah Quaid-E-Azam
Lahore 54000   Tel. (42) 353.601
                         Telefax: (42) 231.730

PHILIPPINE – PHILIPPINES
International Book Center
5th Floor, Filipinas Life Bldg.
Ayala Avenue
Metro Manila   Tel. 81.96.76
                        Telex 23312 RHP PH

PORTUGAL
Livraria Portugal
Rua do Carmo 70-74
Apart. 2681
1200 Lisboa   Tel. (01) 347.49.82/5
                       Telefax: (01) 347.02.64

SINGAPORE – SINGAPOUR
Gower Asia Pacific Pte Ltd.
Golden Wheel Building
41, Kallang Pudding Road, No. 04-03
Singapore 1334   Tel. 741.5166
                       Telefax: 742.9356

SPAIN – ESPAGNE
Mundi-Prensa Libros S.A.
Castelló 37, Apartado 1223
Madrid 28001   Tel. (91) 431.33.99
                       Telefax: (91) 575.39.98

Libreria Internacional AEDOS
Consejo de Ciento 391
08009 – Barcelona   Tel. (93) 488.30.09
                           Telefax: (93) 487.76.59

Llibreria de la Generalitat
Palau Moja
Rambla dels Estudis, 118
08002 – Barcelona
                (Subscripcions) Tel. (93) 318.80.12
                (Publicacions) Tel. (93) 302.67.23
                           Telefax: (93) 412.18.54

SRI LANKA
Centre for Policy Research
c/o Colombo Agencies Ltd.
No. 300-304, Galle Road
Colombo 3   Tel. (1) 574240, 573551-2
                        Telefax: (1) 575394, 510711

SWEDEN – SUÈDE
Fritzes Customer Service
S–106 47 Stockholm   Tel. (08) 690.90.90
                           Telefax: (08) 20.50.21

Subscription Agency/Agence d'abonnements :
Wennergren-Williams Info AB
P.O. Box 1305
171 25 Solna   Tel. (08) 705.97.50
                          Telefax: (08) 27.00.71

SWITZERLAND – SUISSE
Maditec S.A. (Books and Periodicals - Livres
et périodiques)
Chemin des Palettes 4
Case postale 266
1020 Renens VD 1   Tel. (021) 635.08.65
                           Telefax: (021) 635.07.80

Librairie Payot S.A.
4, place Pépinet
CP 3212
1002 Lausanne   Tel. (021) 341.33.47
                           Telefax: (021) 341.33.45

Librairie Unilivres
6, rue de Candolle
1205 Genève   Tel. (022) 320.26.23
                           Telefax: (022) 329.73.18

Subscription Agency/Agence d'abonnements :
Dynapresse Marketing S.A.
38 avenue Vibert
1227 Carouge   Tel. (022) 308.07.89
                           Telefax: (022) 308.07.99

See also – Voir aussi :
OECD Publications and Information Centre
August-Bebel-Allee 6
D-53175 Bonn (Germany)   Tel. (0228) 959.120
                           Telefax: (0228) 959.12.17

THAILAND – THAÏLANDE
Suksit Siam Co. Ltd.
113, 115 Fuang Nakhon Rd.
Opp. Wat Rajbopith
Bangkok 10200   Tel. (662) 225.9531.
                           Telefax: (662) 222.518

TURKEY – TURQUIE
Kültür Yayinlari Is-Türk Ltd. Sti.
Atatürk Bulvari No. 191/Kat 13
Kavaklidere/Ankara   Tel. 428.11.40 Ext. 245
Dolmabahce Cad. No. 29
Besiktas/Istanbul   Tel. (312) 260 7188
                           Telex: (312) 418 29 4

UNITED KINGDOM – ROYAUME-UNI
HMSO
Gen. enquiries   Tel. (171) 873 849
Postal orders only:
P.O. Box 276, London SW8 5DT
Personal Callers HMSO Bookshop
49 High Holborn, London WC1V 6HB
                           Telefax: (171) 873 841
Branches at: Belfast, Birmingham, Bristol,
Edinburgh, Manchester

UNITED STATES – ÉTATS-UNIS
OECD Publications and Information Center
2001 L Street N.W., Suite 650
Washington, D.C. 20036-4910 Tel. (202) 785.6323
                           Telefax: (202) 785.0350

VENEZUELA
Libreria del Este
Avda F. Miranda 52, Aptdo. 60337
Edificio Galipán
Caracas 106   Tel. 951.1705/951.2307/951.1297
                           Telegram: Libreste Caracas

Subscription to OECD periodicals may also be
placed through main subscription agencies.

Les abonnements aux publications périodiques de
l'OCDE peuvent être souscrits auprès des
principales agences d'abonnement.

Orders and inquiries from countries where Distribu-
tors have not yet been appointed should be sent to:
OECD Publications Service, 2 rue André-Pascal,
75775 Paris Cedex 16, France.

Les commandes provenant de pays où l'OCDE n'a
pas encore désigné de distributeur peuvent être
adressées à : OCDE, Service des Publications,
2, rue André-Pascal, 75775 Paris Cedex 16, France.

7-1995

PRINTED IN FRANCE

•

OECD PUBLICATIONS
2, rue André-Pascal
75775 PARIS CEDEX 16
No. 48213
(10 95 40 1) ISBN 92-64-14629-6
ISSN 0376-6438

•